# SYM

CW01429971

**Charles Thomas Taylor**

**Hamilton Books**
A member of
The Rowman & Littlefield Publishing Group
Lanham · Boulder · New York · Toronto · Oxford

Copyright © 2006 by
**Hamilton Books**
4501 Forbes Boulevard
Suite 200
Lanham, Maryland 20706
Hamilton Books Acquisitions Department (301) 459-3366

PO Box 317
Oxford
OX2 9RU, UK

Library of Congress Control Number: 2005939246
ISBN-13: 978-0-7618-3442-7 (paperback : alk. paper)
ISBN-10: 0-7618-3442-7 (paperback : alk. paper)

# Contents

# Preface

Three years ago, when I attempted to renew the call for world federalism with my third book, *Toward World Sovereignty* (University Press of America, Lanham, MD), I recognized that a world unified under democracy must rest upon two secure foundations: first, a rational foundation and then, embedded within and superimposed upon the first, a moral foundation. It almost immediately became clear to me that the first foundation could be nothing other than modern empiricism, long-established in the West since the times of the Scientific Revolution and the Age of Enlightenment and rapidly gaining ascendence today throughout much of the remainder of the world. But what about the moral foundation? It increasingly became clear to me that the second foundation somehow was already in place but that its features would need to be carefully delineated and its irrational roots in religion cautiously extracted. The present work, my fourth book, is an earnest attempt to fulfill both of these requirements.

The present work is an essential recapitulation, development, expansion and reformulation of the two moral philosophies championed in my two earliest books. The three chapters dealing with the principle of beneficial reciprocity, the philosophy of reciprocitarianism and the concept of universal benevolence represent a full exposition of certain subjective ethical values which were introduced and advanced in my first book, *The Values*. The three chapters which address the principle of utility, the philosophy of utilitarianism and the concept of universal law represent a full exposition of the objective elements within the philosophy of utilitarianism. These include the preeminent political and economic ideologies (democracy and regulated capitalism) that have gradually emerged in modern civilization as concrete expressions of these elements. The benefits of such elements, the formulative components of "public utility," were acknowledged and endorsed in my second book, *Person and Society*. The remaining two chapters (I and VIII), which concern the principles and the ethics of noninjury and magnanimity, are the product of a more recent effort to amplify and to refine the initial bipartite core for a plausible and practicable universal moral philosophy.

I wish to thank Marie Ajour and Dana Mendell for their indispensable assistance during the course of preparing my manuscript for publication.

Charles Thomas Taylor
Denver, Colorado, September 12, 2005

# Introduction

I propose to begin this discussion in a rather unconventional manner. In an honest effort to appeal to as many open minds as may be possible, concededly under the risk of initially offending a few of the more intellectually demanding among their number, I would like to advance the central proposition of this work, along with its underlying rationale, through a diction which should be at once most simple, general, and self-evident. To accomplish this preliminary objective, I will proceed dialectically, attempting to answer the obvious questions of those who I can imagine might be the most articulate among my readers.

The first of their questions, "Who are you?" My reply, "I am an American thinker, writing at the beginning of the twenty-first century, who has a strong interest in moral philosophy because neither the problems it raises nor the solutions it provides are adequately addressed or offered in any other academic discipline or vehicle of cultural expression. By thinking, I can define my problem and identify an optimal solution among a number of possibilities. I think because I am a human being, that is, a rational animal. Although reason is one of a number of faculties of the human mind, along with the physiological urges or drives, instinct or intuition, emotion, imagination, memory, and will, it is the highest faculty, that which most clearly distinguishes man from all other animals and has allowed man to dominate all other living beings and to master his natural environment. Accordingly, I can only rely upon the fruit of human thought to solve such problems which may remain or emerge to prevent or to impede human happiness or which may even threaten the very existence of all living beings."

The second of the questions, "What is it that you wish to talk to us about?" My reply, "The moral foundation of a unified world."

Third, "Why discuss the moral foundation of a unified world when the world is not yet unified?" "Because the continuing survival of the human species, and indeed, of all forms of life within our biosphere, and continuing improvement in human well-being, in other words, the forward course of biological evolution, will require a unified world, and furthermore, a world which must become unified in the not-too-distant future. However, the world will not long remain unified, even once unification has been accomplished, without the foundation of a common morality."

Fourth, "Since the five major world religions are immensely diverse and, in certain respects, even somewhat contradictory, how is it that one house for mankind can be built upon a solid moral foundation?" "The moral foundation of a unified world will not derive from religions because religions are the cultural expressions of particular human experiences, attitudes, and suppositions. Furthermore, religion essentially originated not in the highest faculty of the human mind but in emotion and imagination; it was sustained by memory and will. In its most advanced forms, the forms which have endured to the present day, religion almost certainly introduced and developed its highest values and ideals through the power of individual or collective reason although it never fully succeeded in casting off its irrational origins. On the other hand, a universal morality, the solid moral foundation for the house of mankind, must derive totally and exclusively from that which is common to all of mankind, from that unique mental faculty which distinguishes man from all of the other animals, that is, from reason."

Finally, "So you wish to talk to us about a moral philosophy which can serve as a moral foundation for a unified world?" "Quite so, and one which not only can help us to know how best to act toward each other but toward all of the other species of living beings upon the survival and thriving of which our own future security and well-being must inevitably depend. Furthermore, this moral philosophy admittedly is not my unique creation but a synthesis and, in part, a more fully rational development of certain ethics which originated in various earlier philosophies and/or established religions throughout the world. All elements of the ethics are common to certain religious and/or philosophical traditions of both the West and the East, although one element may have received a greater emphasis in the West, another in the East. Most elements are predicated upon common sense and all are universally comprehensible. For all of these reasons, I believe that they should admirably serve their intended purpose."

Having established that our discussion is essentially an original offering of moral philosophy, albeit one somewhat more synthetic than creative, but nonetheless one conceived with the possibility of the greatest consequence for humanity, I should like to proceed with an expositional overview of the philosophy, to be immediately followed with some specific personal observations with respect to the future of moral philosophy as the focal component within a multidisciplinary effort to influence and to modify, if not to determine, human conduct. In the body of the discussion, I will enter into a thorough analysis of each of the four elements of the philosophy, including a full discussion of the underlying principles and relevant institutions which can be identified with each one. I will conclude with a synthetic treatment of the ethics and I will offer some general personal observations with respect to the future of religion and philosophy. Before all of this, however, we will need to consider our current position in the development of reason; to acknowledge where philosophy has led us and to decide whether it is capable, or the extent to which it may be capable, of leading us into the future; to determine precisely what we do, or do not, or can, or can not, know; to recognize the evolution of reason out of nature and to understand that, where human affairs are concerned, the primeval age of the law of nature has recently and abruptly been transformed into the age of the law of reason; and finally, to identify the current categories of knowledge and the relevant disciplines within science and philosophy. These preliminary analyses should help us to establish a basis for concerted thought and practice since we should quickly see that we have passed beyond native common sense to arrive at a level of universal understanding. They should also provide us a rational context to support the presentation of our moral philosophy.

Today, in the West and throughout the greater part of the world, we have come to expect that that which we "know" must be demonstrably certain, or, if not certain, then at least as highly probable as it may be possible to establish. Otherwise, the concepts in or of our minds can not be admissible as knowledge. This expectation arose with the triumph of empiricism in epistemology since the beginning of modern history. The etymology of the term "empiricism" leads us to the Greek word *empeiria*, meaning "experience" or "experiment." In empiricism, we maintain that our knowledge is essentially attained through our experience of sensory perceptions, not through our discovery or recognition of ideas which may (although, for all we know, they just as well may not) already preexist in our minds. Such knowledge so derived from experience can then be identified, organized, and clarified through the mental processes of mathematics and logic.

Empiricism has its roots in ancient Greek philosophy, particularly in the thought of Thales and Aristotle. Aristotle, in attempting to lay out all that is, or can be, known, classified his philosophical works in five great categories: first, the *Organum*, or Logic, which establishes the correct methodology for effective reasoning; second, the Physics and Metaphysics (the Physics, which describes the forms and substance of the phenomena of reality, or of the cosmos, and the Metaphysics, which discusses "first principles," or a hypothesis for the origin of the cosmos); third, biology and psychology; fourth, ethics and politics; and fifth, aesthetics. The second category, without the Metaphysics, the third, and the fourth, without ethics, comprise the earliest systematic attempt to organize and to present that kind of knowledge which is now included in modern science.

Many centuries later, empiricism emerged from its Thalian and Aristotelian cocoon during the Scholasticism of the Middle Ages. Its essential principle was succinctly expressed in the aphorism: *"Nihil est in intellectu quod non prius fuerit in sensu."* In the early seventeenth century, empiricism developed further with the thought of Francis Bacon in England. In his *Novum Organum* of 1620, Bacon transcended the original *Organum* of Aristotle to offer an improved methodology of logic predicated upon a deliberate and direct observation, or sensory experience, of physical phenomena. The most comprehensive and compelling articulation of empiricism occurred seventy years later in 1690 with the publication, also in England, of John Locke's *Essay Concerning Human Understanding*. This date signifies the beginning of the ascendence of the law of reason over the law of nature with respect to human affairs in the course of biological evolution.

Under empiricism, no hypothesis can ever be accepted as generally valid until it has first been thoroughly tested and the conclusions of the test incontrovertibly affirmed. This is the object of the scientific method which presently underlies all of modern science.

In Western philosophy, "empiricism" is commonly contrasted with "rationalism." In rationalism, we maintain that our knowledge is essentially attained through reason itself, irrespective of subsequent confirmation through our perceptions. However, the rise of empiricism does not necessarily signify the fall of rationalism; rather, empiricism becomes required for the ultimate test of rationalism. Not only the conclusions but the premises of the arguments of rationalism must be confirmed by experience; otherwise, the arguments, however eloquent and intriguing, will be specious and useless. To understand more clearly how this should be so, let us pause momentarily to consider the mental process by which a simple idea, or a comprehensive system of ideas, arises in our consciousness.

Let us submit that our original ideas form in the imagination, either as recollected dreams or, more commonly, as daydreams. Our dreams, in particular, may be fragmentary, disjointed, and perplexing. Through reason, we are able to organize our dreams and/or daydreams and to present them as ideas or systems of ideas. Through reason, we become able to create a hypothesis or a theory. In the past, people would accept such a theory as certain knowledge to the extent that the theory would appear to be plausible, that it satisfied certain fundamental emotional needs, and that it was presented by an authority commonly respected both for strength of intellect and eloquence of communication. At the present, we will accept such a theory only as possible or probable but not as certain knowledge unless it has been proven with incontrovertible evidence. Empiricism, then, does not destroy rationalism but perfects it (in much the same manner that a mixed capitalistic economic system does not destroy laissez-faire capitalism but perfects it). Let us attempt to clarify more precisely the distinction between rationalism and empiricism by using an example.

We know that life has existed on earth for more than three billion years. Earth is the third planet from the sun and one of the nine known planets within our solar system. We believe that life probably does not exist on any of the other eight planets of the solar system, for any of three possible reasons: the planet may be too close to the sun so that the planet's atmosphere may be too hot to sustain life, or the planet may be too far so that its atmosphere is too cold; the planet may be too small so that its gravitational force is too weak, or too large so that its gravity is too strong; or the planet may not have the right kinds of matter and energy to create and to sustain life. On the other hand, we know that the sun is one of approximately one hundred billion stars which comprise our galaxy, the Milky Way, and that the Milky Way is one of approximately a half billion galaxies which comprise the universe and are currently accessible to our strongest telescopes. Among all of these stars, a given portion have planets which are very much like the earth: planets each of which is at the right distance from the star around which it orbits, which are of the right size, and which have the right chemicals and energy, to sustain life, and so life seems likely to exist on at least some of these planets. To this point, our thinking has remained in the world of rationalism since it has relied primarily on logic. Accordingly, our knowledge of life on other planets remains suppositional but uncertain. When we become able to send a spacecraft to explore some of these planets so that we are able to obtain sensory experience of the phenomenon of life on one or another of the planets, our thinking will have entered the world of empiricism since it will have come to rely primarily upon experience. Accordingly, to the extent that we succeed in discovering the presence of life on one of these planets, our knowledge of life on another planet will become certain.

Now, there are many noumena which have no relative phenomena. In Western philosophy, these kinds of noumena have been traditionally conceived and developed under rationalism but not empiricism. A few examples of such noumena include idealism; the presence of an ultimate reality other than, or beyond, phenomena; the existence of the soul as an entity apart and distinct from the mind; the existence of spirits outside of the body; the transmigration of the soul; the existence of God; the continuation of life after death; the suspension or reversal of time; and the unerring prediction of future events. Since these noumena provide nothing which, as yet, can ever be experienced by our senses, we have no rational basis to affirm them. This is not to say, of course, that these noumena are not present in our imaginations or that we have no emotional need to affirm them, only that they can never comprise serious, worthy, and valid objects of rational thought.

With the triumph of empiricism in epistemology at the end of the seventeenth century, mankind passed out of the age of the law of nature and into the age of the law of reason. Indeed, the eighteenth century has deservedly been called "the Age of Enlightenment." As a matter of fact, the age of the law of nature, which commenced with the origin of life upon the earth and still persists for all of the lower species of life, will also continue to persist for mankind, coincident to and overlapping the age of the law of reason, until warfare has been universally and permanently outlawed in human society. In broad terms, the age of the law of nature may briefly be described as, borrowing an appropriate phrase from Herbert Spencer, the age of "the survival of the fittest." The age of the law of reason may perhaps best be understood as the age of the ascendence of man. The triumph of empiricism provided the intellectual foundation for the ascendence and globalization of scientific technology throughout modern history. This development has allowed man to satisfy the needs of survival. A parallel development of equal significance has been the ascendence of the universal over the particular in human self-consciousness. This development will allow man to learn to share the means to survive. It will lead to the political, economic, and cultural unification of the world. It will also provide the moral foundation for such a unification.

We are now prepared to identify the current categories of knowledge and the relevant disciplines within science and philosophy which have emerged with the ascendence of empiricism in epistemology. In a large sense, they are simply refinements of the categories of knowledge which Aristotle delineated more than twenty-three hundred years ago. They include the natural sciences: mathematics, astronomy, geology, biology, medicine, chemistry, and physics. Each of these major divisions of natural science has a number of subdivisions. For example, biology includes taxonomy, ecology, anatomy, embryology, histology, cytology, genetics, biochemistry, biophysics, and biogeography. The last three of these subdivisions of biology are interdisciplinary sciences: one an interaction of biology with chemistry; another, with physics; and the last, with geography. The categories of knowledge also include the social, or behavioral, sciences: anthropology, history, psychology, sociology, economics, political science, and law. Each of these major divisions of the social sciences also has a number of subdivisions. Universal agreement on the subdivisions of the social sciences is not as certain as that on the subdivisions of the natural sciences since the social sciences are much more recent and they essentially focus on the study of human beings and human behavior. At this point, we should mention the science of geography, which describes the earth's surface and draws upon elements from both the natural sciences and the social sciences. For example, a map showing the major climatic zones of the world draws upon a natural science (climatology) while a map of the nations of the world draws upon certain of the social sciences (sociology, political science, and history). The categories of knowledge also include, in addition to linguistics (a subdivision of cultural anthropology), languages and the fine arts: literature, theater, cinema, music, dance, and the visual arts. Furthermore, applied arts are widely distributed among numerous professions, trades, industries, and commercial activities. Finally, the categories of knowledge include philosophy, or rather that which remains of philosophy, since philosophy has been dismembered and all except three of its branches reallocated to the sciences and arts: logic, to mathematics; cosmology, where empirically considered, to astronomy and the other natural sciences or, where not, to literature, along with mythology and the sacred scriptures of religion; and ontology, where empirically considered, to psychology or, where not, to literature. Epistemology, ethics and aesthetics remain. Presently, we will have a little more to say concerning the immediate future of ethics. Beforehand, however, let us proceed to introduce, by

way of a brief summary, that moral philosophy which we have proclaimed from the start, which is so rational as to be comprehensible and
acceptable by everyone everywhere and which is most apt and able to
serve as the moral foundation of a unified world.

The philosophy of which we speak is an ethics which will not only
enable the more than six billion persons who currently populate our earth
to live together in peace, harmony, and happiness but it will protect, sustain, and assist all of the other beneficial forms of life upon which human
survival and well-being is, and must continue to be, dependent. We can
refer to this ethics as the philosophy of symbiosism, designating the universal principles of human behavior for living together in security and
happiness, not only as the highest species of life but as caretakers to all
of the other beneficial species of life. The essence of symbiosism is the
sensibility and condition of mutual dependency among human beings.
Ultimately, it must provide the optimal ethics for the great majority of
human beings. It will stand in marked contrast to the ethics of the minority, whether that of any self-sufficient solitudinarian or self-debasing
cadger.

The philosophy of symbiosism rests upon four principles. The first
and second of these are objective and are binding upon all human beings.
The third and fourth principles are subjective and may or may not be
adopted by every human being. All of the principles are essential for
human survival and well-being.

The first principle insures the security of each person, of each community and society of human beings, of the entire species of human beings, and of the totality of life upon the earth. The first principle of ethics
and the first principle of symbiosism is the principle of noninjury. It enjoins each person to refrain from injuring oneself, any other person, or
any other form of sentient or beneficial life. The principle of noninjury
essentially derives from Eastern philosophy, specifically from the doc-
trine of ahimsa in Hinduism and Buddhism, although it has had, and continues to have, a somewhat limited applicability in Western civilization,
specifically in the medical profession, where practitioners are bound by
oath to adhere to the Hippocratic injunction *"Primum non nocere"*
("First, do no harm") with respect to the care and treatment of their patients.

The second principle not only further insures the security of life on
the earth but also provides for the well-being of both person and society.
It is the principle of utility and it advocates useful activity by individuals
and groups. Conversely, it condemns abusive activity. It is indifferent,
even tolerant, toward seemingly useless activity since such activity may

ultimately prove to be really useful, beneficial, and desirable (as with industrial research to develop new products and processes or with artistic creativity). The principle of utility derives from British moral philosophy, specifically from the philosophy of utilitarianism as formulated by Jeremy Bentham and developed by John Austin, James Mill, and John Stuart Mill. The most effectual applications of utilitarianism are cultural or social: one is political, through democracy; another is economic, through capitalism.

The third principle increases the happiness of each person. This is the principle of beneficial reciprocity and it apprises each person to initiate such behavior in behalf of others as may be likely to elicit reciprocal beneficial behavior from others. The application of this moral principle is deeply subjective; the way that a person may assist, serve, provide for, or care about another may vary widely from one person to another; and the objects of such devotion will typically be limited to one's family, closest friends, and associates. The philosophy of reciprocitarianism is anticipated in the ancient altruistic world religions of Buddhism and Christianity and also in classical Chinese philosophy, specifically in Confucianism and Moism. Although the validity, practicability, and efficacy of the principle of beneficial reciprocity may seem to be self-evident, I will take special care to present the philosophy of reciprocitarianism, by defining the term "reciprocitarianism" and by identifying the essential features of the philosophy, in due course.

The fourth principle ennobles man. It is accessible to all but few will embrace it. It is the principle of magnanimity and it urges one, to the extent that one may be able, to conduct oneself at all times with kindness and generosity toward others, to bear misfortune and hardship with serenity and resolve, and to make sacrifices for worthy ends. Those who can be, and are willing to be, magnanimous will become the great leaders, the creative geniuses, the humanitarians, and the heroes of mankind. The principle of magnanimity derives from the ethics of the ancient Greeks and Chinese, from the virtues extolled by Socrates, Aristotle, and the Stoics, and from the concept of *jen* revealed by Confucius. In ancient times, the principle of magnanimity was essentially an ethical value of the aristocracy and of those gifted persons (males, in almost every instance, whether slaves, commoners, or foreigners) directly engaged in service to the aristocracy. Today, the principle of magnanimity must be accessible to anyone who is willing and able to embrace it and it must remain the highest moral aspiration of us all.

The philosophy of symbiosism, then, rests upon four moral principles: noninjury, utility, beneficial reciprocity, and magnanimity. The sources of these principles in combination are universal. I would now like to offer a few additional comments about each one, one by one, to explain why each should be necessary for symbiosism and why human life can not much longer continue to survive and to thrive if each should not be admitted as an essential component of a universal morality.

We have said that the principle of noninjury not only will insure the security of every human being in the world but of all forms of life on the earth, that is, it will maintain the integrity of our biosphere. With respect to the concept of noninjury, here are a few observations which may be worthwhile to bear in mind.

First, the principle of noninjury is a rational moral principle which can only be binding on rational animals. We must not expect the lower animals to behave like human beings nor human beings to behave like the lower animals. Accordingly, we can not expect sharks to stop killing fish, hawks to stop killing mice, or lions to stop killing wildebeest: we can only hope that human beings will not harm themselves, each other, or even any of the other forms of sentient or beneficial life.

Second, the principles of noninjury or magnanimity will be far more difficult to apply than the principles of utility or beneficial reciprocity but, unlike the principle of magnanimity, with which it should be more than sufficient if one out of a hundred proves able and willing to act upon the principle, the principle of noninjury must be acted upon by every human being. This must be so for two reasons.

Third, the first of these reasons concerns the first of the two forms and manifestations of the ascendence of the law of reason in human evolution, namely, the ascendence and globalization of scientific technology. It is far easier today for one person to kill another, or several others (consider the serial killer or the mass murderer) or for the members of one society to perpetrate the mass destruction of the members of another society, or of several other societies (consider modern genocide or nuclear warfare) than at any time in the past. With the advent of nuclear arms and other weapons of mass destruction, the very continuation of life on the earth, whether human or otherwise, has for once come into question.

Fourth, the second of these reasons concerns the second of the two forms and manifestations of the ascendence of the law of reason in human evolution, namely, the ascendence of the universal over the particular in human self-consciousness. Each person now can conceive of himself or herself along with all other persons as members of a single species, the common species of all human life, the species universally recognized as Homo sapiens. The acknowledgement of this fact infers the equality of all human lives. Accordingly, the rational moral principle which protects the integrity of every human life requires that each human being refrains from injuring any other human being.

Fifth, the interpersonal proscriptions of the ethics of noninjury have been universally recognized throughout history to be so indispensable for social harmony that they have formed the substance of the law. Accordingly, an exception to the principle of noninjury must be allowed for those persons who are engaged in law enforcement. Whether we live, as at the present, in a multifarious world of many nations, some technologically-advanced and some underdeveloped, some democratic and some oligarchical, or, more likely than not, as in the future, in a world unified under one universal democratic federal government (the conception and formation of which must remain our greatest political aspiration), personal security and interpersonal justice within society will require that criminals be apprehended, convicted, and punished. Furthermore, the apprehension and/or punishment of criminals may require that they be injured, under the utilitarian principle that an injury to one must be permitted to prevent certain or probable injury to a greater number. In all events, the conditions under which law enforcement officers may inflict injury to suspected or convicted criminals must always be prescribed by law.

Sixth, we have said that the principle of noninjury not only enjoins one to refrain from injuring others but to refrain from self-destruction or from injuring any form of sentient or beneficial life. A full discussion of the situations in which a person may inflict injury to himself or herself, particularly of the problem of suicide, is largely irrelevant to our present purpose and is too complex to introduce until a later time. On the other hand, we will do well to offer some preliminary remarks as to what it must mean to refrain from inflicting injury to the lower forms of life.

Seventh, the extension of the principle of noninjury to include among the objects of its application sentient beings other than human beings has long been practiced in Hindu and Buddhist ethics and has lately been supported in the West by such diverse thinkers as John Stuart Mill (in *Utilitarianism*) and Albert Schweitzer (in *Reverence for Life*). The argument, of course, arises out of a feeling of compassion and concern for all forms of life which are able to experience the sensation of pain. Furthermore, I would argue that by enlarging one's scope of compassion to include all, or at least some, of the other forms of life, one's sensitivity to the needs and feelings of all, or at least most, other human beings will tend to increase in proportion. In the cases of Hinduism and Buddhism, there is a kind of human identification with the lower forms of life because of the strong and enduring belief in the transmigration of souls.

Apart from Hinduism and Buddhism, especially in the West, there is a kind of sensibility and sympathy for the sensations and feelings experienced by animals, particularly those of the more advanced species which possess the most highly-developed brains and nervous systems. Two problems which can be associated with this concern for all forms of sentient life require recognition.

Eighth, the first of these two problems, of course, is for us to determine just how far down the phylogenetic tree we must reach in extending the principle of noninjury. Any attempt to solve this problem in the course of formulating a universal morality will raise many ethical questions and suggest many fundamental changes in attitudes and customs, particularly in the West. For example, we must ask "Should we become vegetarians? Should we no longer use fur in our wearing apparel? Should we give up hunting and fishing for sport?" We must wait until a little later to address this problem and to attempt to provide satisfactory, definitive, and universally-binding answers to these questions.

Ninth, the second of the two problems associated with compassion and concern for sentient life is the conflict which arises when an attempt to improve human well-being involves the infliction of injury to animals. We are referring, of course, to the use of animals in medical research. We must ask "Will we be justified to grant an exception to the broadest practicable extension of the principle of noninjury where the sacrifice of the lives or well-being of animals in medical research can save human lives or improve human well-being?" As with the previous problem and the questions it raises, we will do best to wait until later to address this problem and to answer this question.

Tenth, the extension of the principle of noninjury to include among the objects of its application not only as many forms of sentient life as may be proper and practicable but all forms of beneficial life (meaning all forms of life that are necessary and beneficial for human life) creates one of the fundamental principles which support the modern social movement and political policy of environmentalism. In the future, as at the present, we must largely rely upon assistance from the science of ecology to guide our ethical behavior in this area. A thorough discussion of the theory of environmentalism will complete our presentation of the first principle of symbiosism.

We have said that the principle of utility not only further insures the security (which is to say, the very survival) of life on the earth but also provides for the well-being of humanity, whether "humanity" should be conceived of as an aggregation of autonomous individuals or as a homogeneous social whole. As articulated by the British utilitarians, the principle of utility asserts that that action is best which creates or increases the happiness of the greatest number or, stated conversely, which prevents or decreases the unhappiness of the greatest number. To try to understand a little more clearly the meaning of this definition, let us examine its two most authoritative sources: first, the definition provided by Jeremy Bentham and, second, the one provided by John Stuart Mill.

While utilitarianism has deep roots in ancient Greek philosophy, specifically in the thought of Socrates and Epicurus, it was introduced in a fully developed form during modern times by Jeremy Bentham in 1781 with his book *The Principles of Morals and Legislation*. In chapter one, "Of the Principle of Utility," Bentham writes:

> By the principle of utility is meant that principle which approves or disapproves of every action whatsoever, according to the tendency which it appears to have to augment or diminish the happiness of the party whose interest is in question: or, what is the same thing in other words, to promote or to oppose that happiness. I say of every action whatsoever; and therefore not only of every action of a private individual, but of every measure of government.
>
> By utility is meant that property in any object, whereby it tends to produce benefit, advantage, pleasure, good, or happiness, (all this in the present case comes to the same thing) or (what comes again to the same thing) to prevent the happening of mischief, pain, evil, or unhappiness to the party whose interest is considered: if that party be the community in general, then the happiness of the community: if a particular individual, then the happiness of that individual.

The moral philosophy of Jeremy Bentham was further developed and greatly refined by John Stuart Mill in 1863 with his forceful essay "Utilitarianism." Using the definition of the principle of utility as his point of departure (as did Bentham), Mill's definition is virtually the same as that of Bentham. In chapter two, "What Utilitarianism Is," he writes:

> The creed which accepts as the foundation of morals *utility*, or the *greatest happiness principle*, holds that actions are right in proportion as they tend to promote happiness, wrong as they tend to produce the reverse of happiness. By 'happiness' is intended pleasure, and the absence of pain; by 'unhappiness,' pain, and the privation of pleasure . . .
>
> According to the 'greatest happiness principle,' as above explained, the ultimate end, with reference to and for the sake of which all other things are desirable (whether we are considering our own good or that of other people), is an existence exempt as far as possible from pain, and as rich as possible in enjoyments, both in point of quantity

and quality; the test of quality, and the rule for measuring it against quantity, being the preference felt by those who in their opportunities of experience, to which must be added their habits of self-consciousness and self-observation, are best furnished with the means of comparison. This, being, according to the utilitarian opinion, the end of human action, is necessarily also the standard of morality; which may accordingly be defined, the rules and precepts for human conduct, by the observance of which an existence such as has been described might be, to the greatest extent possible, secured to all mankind; and not to them only, but, so far as the nature of things admits, to the whole sentient creation . . .

Utility includes not solely the pursuit of happiness, but the prevention or mitigation of unhappiness; and if the former aim be chimerical, there will be all the greater scope and more imperative need for the latter, so long at least as mankind think fit to live, and do not take refuge in the simultaneous act of suicide . . .

We shall soon see how utilitarianism, through democracy, can unify the world under one social contract, one government, and one code of universal law to establish permanent peace, thereby insuring the personal security of everyone everywhere. We shall also see how utilitarianism, through free-fair capitalism, can provide a universal economy, supported and guided by a world democratic federal government, to improve the general prosperity of mankind.

It should not be too difficult to understand why the principle of utility is indispensable for symbiosism. Symbiosism offers the prototypical universal ethics for the only species of life that has, at long last, attained a general consciousness of itself as a species and of its intraspecific interdependency. The ascendence of the age of the law of reason over the age of the law of nature in human affairs, which is to say, the triumph of reason over unreason, is revealed not only by the rise of science and technology but by the rise of universalism, which is to say, by the triumph of human self-consciousness over class, racial, religious, regional, or national self-consciousness, of democracy over oligarchy in all of its forms, and of free-fair capitalism over slavery, seignorialism, mercantilism, and socialism. Since the maximal extent of "the greatest number" of the principle of utility neither can be greater than nor must be no fewer than the totality of mankind, that is, the entire population of the world, only that ethics which espouses the happiness of the greatest number can serve as an appropriate active objective ethics for mankind. Therefore, utilitarianism is necessary for symbiosism and for the optimal progress of the human species.

We have said that the principle of beneficial reciprocity increases the happiness of each person. We have also said that the principles of beneficial reciprocity and magnanimity are subjective, in contradistinction to the principles of noninjury and utility, which are objective. Before we offer any additional comments on each of the subjective principles, we will do best first to explain why the philosophy of symbiosism requires that some parts of its ethics must be objective while other parts must be subjective.

Let us begin by revisiting the definition of ethics. Ethics is the branch of philosophy which is concerned with determining what is good and bad, or right and wrong, in human behavior; it is likewise concerned with determining personal and social rights and obligations. Since human beings are social animals, most of our actions tend to affect other people. In his intriguing book, *Sociobiology* (1975, first edition; 1980, abridged edition), Frank B. Baird, Jr. of Harvard University, writing under the pseudonym Edward O. Wilson, has argued that over the course of evolution, four groups of animals have achieved extraordinary levels of social organization: the colonial invertebrates, the social insects, the nonhuman mammals, and man. He has observed that the earlier and more primitive the group, the higher the degree of social cohesion and the lower the degree of individuation. (Accordingly, man should have the lowest degree of social cohesion and the highest degree of individuation.) Nevertheless, Baird notes that while man has attained a high degree of individuation, man does not exhibit a low degree of social cohesion. On the contrary, the social cohesion of human beings is greater than that of the other mammals and it approaches or surpasses that of the social insects in one respect or another. Baird maintains that man has been successful in reversing the downward trend in social evolution because of his superior intelligence, a conclusion which is highly compatible with my own assertion that we live during that overlapping period when the age of the law of reason, with respect to human affairs, begins to supersede the age of the law of nature.

We need to bear in mind, then, that the human species has a high degree not only of individuation but of social cohesion. Man exists both as person and society. Man's behavior must be considered in the combination of two opposing perspectives: the sociological and the psychological. Accordingly, a complete system of universal ethics must accommodate both the objective and the subjective.

Throughout history, almost all known systems of ethics have been objective, designed to create a perfect society by inducing individuals to behave in conformity with some general standard of behavior. Objective ethics, then, whether deriving from religion or philosophy, would have arisen as an attempt to raise the degree of social cohesion in ancient man. The ethics of symbiosism should further raise the degree of social cohesion in modern man through the universal observance and application of the principles of noninjury and utility.

On the other hand, the ethics of symbiosism acknowledges that a higher degree of social cohesion can never be achieved at the cost of a lower degree of human individuation, which is to say, that a more secure, functional, and harmonious society, especially one which must transform into a universal society, can not be accomplished at the cost of personal happiness and self-actualization. Therefore, a portion of the ethics of symbiosism must be subjective, such that although the general meaning of such an ethics may be widely understood, the scope and degree of the application of the ethics will tend to vary greatly from one individual to another, according to the direction and strength of personal concern, motivation, and inclination. The direct object of subjective ethics is to create a benefit not for society as a whole but for an individual, any given individual, possibly, even hopefully, but not necessarily, each and every individual within society.

Under the risk of being largely, or even completely, misunderstood (a risk for which I am willing to accept total responsibility, since the source of the fault, if a fault should arise, will certainly be traced to the writer's miscommunication rather than the reader's misconception), I should like to suggest that the roots of subjective ethics in Western philosophy can be derived from Socrates and the Socratic injunction: "*Gnothi seauton*"; from Pascal and the insights revealed in his magnum opus, *Les Pensées*; and from the recent emergence of existentialism during the past one and a half centuries with the thought of Kierkegaard, Nietsche, Jaspers, Heideggar, and Sartre. In my opinion, the existentialists achieved three monumental interrelated objectives: one, the refutation of continental rationalism and Platonic idealism; two, the construction of an intellectual bridge linking the new existentialist thought of continental Europe with the empirical and pragmatic thought of Britain and America; and three, the affirmation that an understanding of the nature and meaning of human existence requires a full examination and understanding of all of the various components and workings of the human mind in all of its multifarious gradations of consciousness, a penetrating study not only of cognition, intellectual creativity, and reason but of sensation, perception, the drives, the emotions, the will, memory, imagination, intuition, and instinct. Although the ethical implications of existentialism are immense, the nineteenth century existentialists ex-

pended the greater portion of their creative energies in religious icono-
clasm; the twentieth century existentialists, in ontology. Nevertheless,
existentialism remains essentially humanistic and immeasurably optimis-
tic. The single greatest contribution of existentialist thought resides in the
powerful argument that each person is free to create the meaning of his
or her own life and that each person is solely responsible for his or her
own actions, for what he or she does to, or for, other people, and, to a
very large extent, for the way that other people act toward, or in behalf
of, himself or herself. To the extent that existentialism becomes increasingly compatible with empiricism, its influence on the formation and development of the subjective ethics of symbiosism should be quite profound.

The essence of the principles of noninjury and beneficial reciprocity
is embodied in the Golden Rule, articulated, first, in negative form by
Confucius, "Do not do to others what you would not like others to do to
you," and, second, in positive form by Jesus, "Do to others what you
would like others to do to you." It is not by accident that consciousness
of this quintessential moral principle first emerged in negative form. It is
the essence of the principle of noninjury, which provides the foundation
for all of the other valid moral principles and without which the further
development of morality would be impossible or futile. The positive
form of the Golden Rule is the essence of the principle of beneficial reciprocity. To the extent that one person shows concern for others, or
helps others, or acts as a friend to others, others are likely to show concern for that person, or to help that person, or to act as friends to that person. In this manner, a person receives assistance in his or her efforts to
satisfy the needs and to mitigate the hurts of life. Furthermore, a person
can secure the optimal means to satisfy his or her sexual urges, that is, to
fulfill his or her genetic destiny, by obtaining a desirable and appropriate
mate and, hopefully, an exclusive, enduring, and intimate friend with
whom to share the risks and rewards of life. The interpersonal relationships which proceed from filiation, marriage, and parenthood provide
sources of some of the greatest happiness which can be experienced in
human existence.

In passing, let us not fail to note that we must forever reject the principle of detrimental reciprocity, aside from the routine operation of justice under the law. Both history and common human experience demonstrate that evil begets evil, malice creates malice, and violence sustains
violence. Therefore, we must overcome nature with reason and impulse
with deliberation. We can only withstand anger with equanimity and
anxiety with tranquility. In our social and political relationships, we must

move as quickly as possible to establish and to maintain a just and secure world. In our interpersonal relationships, we will always do best to face evil with good, malice with benevolence, and violence with noninjury.

We have said that the principle of magnanimity ennobles man. Throughout the past, in an almost completely oligarchical world, magnanimity was the highest ethical value of the aristocracy. Throughout the future, in a completely, or almost completely, democratic world, magnanimity must be the highest ethical value of humanity.

The principle of magnanimity is the optimal personal application of the principle of utility since it attempts either to create a benefit for the greatest number (as when a wealthy man bequeaths his fortune to serve as an endowment for some nonprofit institution that provides resources for the disadvantaged or services for the general public) or to prevent or to mitigate a detriment to the greatest number (as when a person who "just happens to be at the right place at the right time" steps forward with little or no thought for his or her personal safety to prevent, or to give warning of, an impending crime or natural disaster, or to rescue the victims of a crime or natural disaster). Despite the obvious relationship between utility and magnanimity, we must recognize a fundamental distinction between these two ethical principles: utility never requires a person to sacrifice his or her personal security and/or well-being for the sake of the greatest number (even where a person has chosen an occupation which directly provides security for the general public, such as a member of the national armed forces or of a municipal or provincial police or fire department) while magnanimity always requires a person to place the personal security and/or well-being of the greatest number ahead of his or her personal security and/or well-being, or the well-being of his or her family and closest friends. Let us recapitulate. The principle of noninjury requires that one will not be abusive. The principle of utility recommends that one disengage from useless activity and practice primarily that which is useful. The principle of beneficial reciprocity proposes that each person care about other people. The principle of magnanimity requires either that one practice that which is useful, or care about the safety and comfort of other people, to such an extent that one deny oneself, and possibly even one's family and closest friends, for the well-being of a greater number of other people, or that one sacrifice one's own existence for the existence and happiness of other people.

There are two forms in which a person can exercise the principle of magnanimity. The first of these requires that a person wields considerable power and/or influence or commands enormous resources of wealth. This form is either what we commonly call "humanitarianism" (after the

Latin) or "philanthropy" (after the Greek). While the denotations of the two terms are roughly equivalent, the connotative use of the term "humanitarian" suggests a person (like Jeremy Bentham or Albert Schweitzer) who effectively promotes social reform or human welfare, especially in behalf of the underprivileged or disadvantaged persons within an advanced society or all of the members of a primitive and/or underdeveloped society, while the connotative use of the term "philanthropist" suggests a person (like Alfred Bernhard Nobel or Andrew Carnegie) who effectively contributes a substantial personal fortune for the welfare of the uneducated, the sick, and the poor or for the common benefit of society as a whole. Since the reallocation of personal wealth to satisfy social needs is essentially a valid function of government in a modern democratic society, we prefer the term "humanitarianism" to the term "philanthropy" and we will use it exclusively henceforth.

Unlike the first form of magnanimity, wherein an individual, whether through personal leadership or wealth, creates a benefit for the greatest number, the second form is one in which a person prevents a disaster, or relieves suffering, for the greatest number. This form is what we commonly call "heroism." Let us comment on three observations with respect to this form. First, there are no special requirements for a person to become a hero or a heroine other than those of self-confidence, personal commitment, ability, and courage. Second, even as the principle of non-injury precedes and underlies the other three principles of symbiosism, so a person's act of preventing, or mitigating, a detriment to humanity, or society, or the greatest number, is more indispensable than that same person's act of creating a benefit for the greatest number. Third, while service as a humanitarian may demand an uncertain measure of self-denial, service as a hero or heroine may exact self-sacrifice. For reasons which flow from these observations, heroism might seem to be the higher form of magnanimity. Yet, it is not. Why should this be so?

It is because of two reasons. First, happiness requires human well-being over and above mere survival or rudimentary subsistence. Therefore, the value of acts of humanitarianism will always at least equal, when it does not surpass, the value of acts of heroism, except where an act of heroism not only preserves human life but an advanced standard of living as well. Second, the humanitarian, acting in deliberation, may devote his entire life in promoting the well-being of humanity, or of a substantial portion of it, rather than, or even at the expense of, his own well-being, or that of his family or closest friends. On the other hand, the hero, typically acting on impulse under the stress of the moment, may become a hero in as little as five minutes but behave in a most unheroic, mundane, and perhaps even ignoble manner during the remaining portion of his life.

One who would become a humanitarian must first have achieved a sufficient measure of personal happiness and worldly success, otherwise he or she will be largely ineffective in advancing a cause greater than that of self-interest or friendship. Accordingly, the way of the humanitarian must become a way of life unto itself. It must remain the highest of all virtues and the ultimate aspiration of the symbiosist.

This concludes our overview of symbiosism. Let us recall that the present discussion is essentially a work of moral philosophy, or ethics, and that its stated purpose is to introduce an ethics suitable to serve as the moral foundation for a unified world. It is necessary that a rational exposition of the universal principles advanced as a guide for human conduct should be presented as ethics (as one of the three remaining branches of philosophy today along with epistemology and aesthetics), rather than as a science or an art. This is so because there is no single science or art to which the ethics of symbiosism could properly be reallocated. It might be possible to reallocate the objective ethics, the ethics of noninjury and utilitarianism, to sociology and the subjective ethics, the ethics of reciprocitarianism and magnanimity (the latter in its forms of heroism and humanitarianism), to psychology, but two problems arise. First, while the humane and environmental components of the ethics of noninjury are clearly sociological, the self-preservation component is essentially psychological. Therefore, a full discussion of the ethics of noninjury would require a reallocation to two disciplines of social science. Second, even if the ethics of noninjury could be entirely reallocated to sociology, the reallocation of the fourfold ethics of symbiosism between two uncoordinated social sciences would destroy the overall unity and organic interrelationships of the ethics. No single social science, not even anthropology, presently exists for the study of the human being both as person and society. Therefore, the presentation of a universal ethics, an ethics which incorporates principles of personal and social conduct and which combines and reconciles objectivity and subjectivity, must remain in philosophy, from which, and as such, it can serve as the singular source of universal personal value and social policy while exerting a powerful and profound influence on the future development of relevant social sciences.

# I.
# The First Principle of Ethics—Noninjury

The first principle of ethics is the principle of noninjury. It is expressed in the maxim, first formulated in ancient Greece 2,400 years ago by Hippocrates for specific application in medical practice, "First, do no harm." Hippocrates intended that his admonition be observed by physicians, who, by virtue of their specialized and thorough knowledge of medicine, possess a singular and covetable power. With the modern ascendence of the universal over the particular, all of us have been becoming aware of the latent, and either fostering or devastating, influence and power which most of us can exert, when circumstances are conducive, over the lives of at least a few other persons. Accordingly, that admonition has now attained relevance far beyond the realm of professional ethics. The subject of this maxim today is every human being; the object is the self of the subject, every other human being, and even every member of every other form of life that is sentient or otherwise necessary for human life.

To understand precisely what it is that we must do, or, more accurately, not do, to comply with the requirement of the principle, we must analyze the act which we must avoid. Now, every act is potentially surrounded by intention and consequence so that, in effect, it becomes either a single, bipartite, or tripartite event. Accordingly, an act may be intentional or unintentional while its consequence may be effective or ineffective. With respect to the act of injuring someone, or some other living thing, a person can not be said to be refraining from the act unless he or she has no intention to act, since the consequences of continuous attempts to carry out an intentional act may not always be ineffective. Neither can a person be said to be refraining from the act, even though it be unintentional, when the consequence of the act is effective. There are two events in which this outcome can arise: one, during an accidental act or, two, during a multilateral act. In either event, the person who performs the act can never be relieved from his or her responsibility for the effective consequence of the act, unless a person who was injured as a consequence of the act has caused the act to occur, whether by intention or not. Let us attempt to explain why this should be so.

In the instance of an accidental act, a person who performs the act may either be negligent or reckless. In the former case, the person has failed to exercise sufficient care in the performance of an act that would ordinarily provide a benefit for the object of the act, with the unintended consequence that injury was sustained by at least one person or other being, whether sentient or otherwise beneficial for human life. In the latter case, the person has failed to exercise sufficient care in the performance of an act that should ordinarily have little or no effect on people or other living things, again with the unintended consequence that injury was somehow sustained by at least one person or other being. In this case, the person performing the act is not engaged in any kind of activity that is intentionally useful for other people, or obviously beneficial for the natural environment, but rather is enjoying recreational or adventurous activity, as in socializing, traveling, practicing a hobby, or participating in a game or sport. In either case, the person who performs an act which causes injury to life, even though unintentional, has failed to provide adequately for the uninterrupted safety and well-being of human beings or other beings that are also sentient, that is, conscious of pleasure and pain, or otherwise beneficial, that is, necessary, for human life, during the course of performing the activities of his or her legitimate occupation or personal recreation. This negligence, or recklessness, is no less blameworthy than a deliberate injurious act.

In the instance of a multilateral act, a person unwillingly performs an unintentional injurious act under the coercion of another person or, more likely, a group of persons. If the person is a willing agent of the principal who intends to act injuriously, then, of course, the agent himself, or herself, is acting intentionally. It does not matter that the principal is the party who conceives, plans, and directs the performance of the act since the performance could not be carried out without the services of the agent. If, on the other hand, the person is an unwilling agent of the principal, then the agent faces a moral dilemma. Either the agent acquiesces and so becomes no less blameworthy than the principal, in the recognition that the consequence of the act of the agent is no different than that which would arise if the act were directly executed by the principal, or the agent refuses to comply with the directions of the principal and so becomes subject as well to the risk of injury by the principal. Now, the current rights and the future security of the injured rely upon the common acceptance of the moral code and the general observance of the law. If neither the moral code nor the law protect the injured from the intentional acts of the injurer, then the unwilling agent of such a principal is confronted with only two alternatives: the agent may either oppose the principal as a hero (and so accept a high risk of becoming injured by the principal) or flee from the locale of the principal, hopefully to arrive at a different locale where the people accept a moral code and maintain a body of law that generally protects the vulnerable from the intentional acts of an injurer and otherwise promptly redresses wrongful injury. If such a locale can not be found and the agent is neither willing nor able to oppose the principal, the agent still has no other choice than to flee from the principal to avoid obvious complicity with respect to a deliberate act that causes injury to life.

If we do not refrain from injuring other people, whether the injury be physical, possessional, or emotional, we will create an interpersonal atmosphere of mistrust that will greatly undermine, and likely even threaten to prevent, the activities of utilitarianism, reciprocitarianism, and humanitarianism. However, we must not fail to acknowledge and to remember that human beings are not gods (those singular creations of the human imagination) but animals. Among animals, herbivores are generally placid, carnivores, violent, at least at such times when they must secure a meal or, for the males, a mate. We say that the typical behavior of animals is "instinctive." Man is an omnivore and, as such, may at certain times be placid and at other times be violent. However, like a lion in a zoo, man has outgrown his need to be violent. At present, we know too little about the human mind and its workings to be able to say with any high degree of probability whether human behavior, whether placid or violent, is instinctive or not and, if so, to what approximate extent. If it is instinctive, there may still be considerable genetic and/or cultural variability among individuals. Accordingly, it may be necessary for all of us to avoid any activities or influences which may lead to violence. It may also be necessary for some of us at least to engage in acts of Freudian sublimation if we are to achieve success in our effort to refrain from injuring other people, or ourselves, or any other forms of sentient or beneficial life.

To understand the activities or influences which we must attempt to avoid because otherwise they may stimulate us to engage in acts of violence, let us consider just what it is that provokes a person to be violent.

Certainly, when one person deliberately injures another, or threatens to injure another, the person who has been injured, or threatened with injury, will become angry and will be inclined to retaliate. This situation is undoubtedly the most direct and common cause of violence. Also, when one person deliberately injures, or threatens to injure, a close relative, friend, or associate of another, the person whose close relative, friend, or associate has been injured, or threatened with injury, will likewise be angry and inclined to retaliate. The same holds true when one person deliberately injures, or threatens to injure, an economic interest of, or a fundamental value or system of values held by, another. In general and to a lesser extent, the same holds true when the injury takes the form of an insult, a belittlement, or a discourtesy, which is to say that the injury is emotional, or psychosocial, rather than physical. In all of these situations, the act, or even the threat, of injury tends to provoke a violent response. Therefore, the proclivity to violence will abate only as the incidence of injury decreases. By way of further support for this argument, consider the contrast between carnivorous animals that live in the wild and those that live in captivity. Those that live in the wild engage in acts of violence repeatedly to secure their food; those that live in captivity, when they are treated well and fed regularly, are docile and seldom engage in acts of violence unless provoked.

At this point, we must raise the question of whether the act of violence, or the semblance of violence, in the fine arts, in the entertainment media, and in the spectator and participatory sports tends to increase or to decrease the incidence of injury caused by human beings? If we subscribe, whether fully or in part, to the Aristotelian theory of catharsis or affirm, whether fully or in part, a primarily didactical function of culture (both as to classical and popular culture), we must answer "decrease!" At any rate, it would seem groundless to postulate a direct causal relationship between vicarious and actual experience, except for those who are mentally ill or whose mental faculties are immature or otherwise very poorly developed. We would anticipate that science will provide a definitive answer to the question after sufficient time has elapsed for conclusive study.

Those of us whose mental faculties are lucid, mature, and adequately developed and whose emotional health is sound may nonetheless need to redirect probable instinctive hostile impulses into constructive channels through useful work that provides a clear benefit for ourselves and for others. To overcome any desire, whether conscious or unconscious, to punish others for past wrongs and inconsiderations, we must throw ourselves, constantly and wholeheartedly, into our constructive projects. At the same time, relying upon the operation of law for the security of our persons and our property, we must forgive all of those who have wronged us and angered us, or who have been indifferent to us at those times when we most needed them for their kindness, friendship, and emotional support. These actions flow from our specific interpretation and intentional application of the prototypical Freudian theory of sublimation. Its ready adoption is cardinal for the thorough and effective practice of the principle of noninjury.

Let us not fail to recognize and to remember that only man can practice sublimation. The lower animals are not capable of this practice. Man can tame the lower animals once he has captured them and placed them in captivity. Then he can condition them to be nonviolent or, at least, less violent. By the same token, man can condition himself, through sublimation, to be nonviolent. It is a process of overcoming nature with reason. It is a process of transforming evil into good.

In his magnum opus, *Being and Time*, Martin Heidegger has said that care is that which is most fundamental to the condition of being of the human being. By virtue of the results from many recent studies of animal behavior, we would further suggest that care may be that which is most fundamental to the condition of being of any sentient being. Now, no one who has seen anything of life can fail to observe that when a human being is hostile to other human beings, or has suffered an injury that was deliberately inflicted upon him or her by some other human being and so becomes himself or herself resentful as a consequence and hostile in due course, the care which that human being manifests will be largely restricted to himself or herself and to the objects and entities which he or she possesses or controls. Care expands, with respect to the number of its specific objects, only as intentional injury, or the fear of intentional injury, diminishes. Care is imprisoned by hostility but liberated by sublimation.

If a sentient being, whether a human being or one of the lower forms of being, has been badly treated, it becomes unhappy: it will become insensitive and ill-tempered toward other sentient beings. Conversely, if the same sentient being has been well treated, it becomes happy: it will become sensitive and well-disposed toward other sentient beings. Through sublimation, to a very large extent, human beings can finally begin to overcome their resentments and hostilities, whether overt or covert, and to avoid inflicting injury upon other sentient beings. With less injury, human suffering decreases. With less human suffering, human happiness increases. With greater human happiness, human sensitivity expands. With greater human sensitivity, human behavior toward all sentient beings, fully or largely, irrespective of species, improves. Throughout this process, destruction gives way to construction and injury to noninjury; unhappiness is transformed into happiness and insensitivity into sensitivity. But what would happen, we must ask, if this felicific course of progress should suddenly come to a stop and then begin to regress? What would happen if the supreme human achievement of universal human sensitivity were ultimately to become undone by lingering attitudes disfavoring sensitivity and by persisting practices of desensitization?

These questions, of course, are rhetorical. It will not be solely sufficient to provide a fundamental and effective support for the practice of noninjury through the practice of sublimation. It will be necessary at the same time to abolish the practice of desensitization. In an attempt both to understand more clearly the problem of the practice of desensitization and to develop a workable and effective solution for the problem, we must address the problem by analyzing the various forms in which the practice of desensitization is usually apparent. There are five such forms, which we can identify as interpersonal discrimination, military training, hazing, hunting, and cruelty in sports.

When we speak of interpersonal discrimination, we mean that we effect a difference in the way that we treat people as based upon our prior evaluation of the characteristics of the groups to which they belong rather than our present evaluation of the merits of their individual accomplishments and reputations. This discrimination is commonly predicated upon such standard societal divisions and population demographics as race, nationality or national origin, religion, age, gender, sexual preference, physical health or physical fitness, education, occupation, wealth, and social class. The sensitivity which one feels for, and shows to, another is fully or largely nullified when the other is a member of a group that is the object of discrimination. If the common opinion with respect to the members of a particular group is one of low regard, mistrust, or contempt, those members are likely to face either becoming dehumanized or even demonized over time. However, since discrimination is essentially unjust, it is prohibited by law in progressive democratic governments. We have argued that the world must soon unite for the sake of lasting security and prosperity. Nations which currently allow discrimination but which desire to become part of the new universal democratic federation must be required to prohibit such discrimination before being admitted into the federation. Accordingly, the problem of desensitization in interpersonal discrimination will become irrelevant under a universal democratic government.

Desensitization is necessary in military training so that soldiers can be conditioned to kill the enemy. As I have argued in an earlier book, *Toward World Sovereignty*, the unification of the world under one common democratic federal government will serve to abolish warfare, to disband national armies, and to enforce permanent disarmament. World peace can be maintained by a relatively small world democratic federal police force. Accordingly, the problem of desensitization in military training will also become irrelevant, or at least much less relevant, under a universal democracy.

Hazing is an archaic and obsolete social practice originating in the rites of passage for male adolescents in primitive societies. Such initiation rites, still practiced in certain parts of the world, as among the Masai of eastern Africa and the Australian aborigines, are intended to commemorate and to assist the transition from boyhood to manhood. The initiate is generally required to endure specific ordeals designed to develop his courage, toughness, and self-reliance so that he will be adequately prepared to assume the responsibilities of adulthood. In advanced societies, the practice persists among the quasi or, more accurately, pseudo aristocracy of the upper socioeconomic classes as a vestige of previous oligarchical societies. It can still be seen in certain schools (preparatory and college) and branches of the military where there is an elitist tradition to take in, develop, and turn out the strongest, brightest and ablest young men. Hazing in schools no longer fulfills functions that are commensurate with those of initiating older boys to the privileges and obligations of manhood in primitive societies or of honing the education and training of the aristocratic class in an oligarchy. On the contrary, desensitization in schools is clearly incompatible with the practice of sublimation, the experience of happiness, and the furtherance of universal human sensitivity. Accordingly, we must reject and condemn the practice of hazing in schools. We would urge that legislation be introduced to prohibit it in whichever advanced societies it may be present. At the same time and for the same reason, we must reject and condemn the practice of hazing in the military.

Hunting is another archaic and obsolete human activity. Once the dangerous but necessary occupation of primitive man, it has evolved into the cruel and needless pastime of modern man. It is thoughtless and heartless to cause useless suffering for other sentient beings, even if their brains are not as advanced and their nervous systems not as developed as those of human beings. The practice of desensitization with respect to the lower species also compromises and hinders, either directly or indirectly, the process of sensitization with respect to our own species. Many ways remain for us to experience the exhilaration of outdoor recreation and the pleasure of natural beauty without inflicting injury upon wild animals in their natural habitat. We would urge that legislation be introduced in every society on earth to prohibit altogether the practice of hunting for sport.

We would offer the same argument with respect to the problem of cruelty in sports, specifically those in which the participants are trained or bred and then presented to fight one another, whether the sport be that of heavyweight boxing or one of those which involve the participation of animals, including bullfighting, cockfights, and dogfights. These kinds of sports are vestiges of ancient, violent, and unknowing civilizations. To watch a sport which features the infliction of injury by one sentient being upon another, irrespective of whether either of the sentient beings is a human being or a member of a lower species of animal life, is as mindless as it would be to witness an injury to a victim of a crime or an accident without attempting in any way to assist the victim. At best, it is an example of misguided and wasted sublimation; at worst, it is an act of complicity, since neither the sport nor its cruelty could occur without the active support of its enthusiasts. As with hunting, and with a similar rationale, we would urge that legislation be introduced in every society on earth to prohibit all forms of cruelty in sports.

In our foregoing preliminary remarks, we have proposed to establish the Hippocratic injunction, "First, do no harm," as the first maxim for all of ethics; we have offered an analysis of action as consisting of an intention (or its absence), an act, and a consequence (whether effective or ineffective) and we have concluded that the consequence of an act is as fully momentous as the intention of the act; we have acknowledged the crucial role of Freudian sublimation in the practice of noninjury; we have recognized the Heideggerian observation that care is central to the being of the human being, we have enlarged the scope of this observation by suggesting that care may indeed be central to the being of all sentient beings, and we have noted a direct causal relationship between the expansion of care (with respect to the number of its specific objects) and the absence of resentment, hostility, and deliberate injury; and we have presented arguments to reject the various lingering practices of desensitization. At this juncture, we are prepared to proceed with a full consideration of care within each of three categories of objects in the practice of noninjury. We will begin with a discussion of the problem of self-destruction.

# 1. Self-Preservation

For as long as any hope for personal happiness abides, each person will practice self-preservation. It is generally when one lacks or loses the courage to endure relentless personal suffering that one conceives the idea of self-destruction.

We remember that man is a rational animal: as such, he is subject at once to the laws of nature and the law of reason. We have said that the typical behavior of animals is "instinctive," meaning that such behavior arises spontaneously without involving reason or will. Perhaps we should say that "instinct," in a human being, is that behavior that is most closely identified with, or related to, the fundamental physiological urges and drives. Now, all animals, including human beings, have a fundamental urge to survive. This "instinct" is most evident in human beings when they are in the earliest stages of life, either during infancy or early childhood, before the capacity for reason has been fully developed. The urge to self-destruct is not typically present among the lower animals, except for specific altruistic purposes, as when a mother cougar sacrifices herself in defending her kittens from the attack of a pack of wolves or a honeybee sacrifices itself in stinging an intruder to the beehive. Neither is the urge to self-destruct typically present among human beings. The idea of self-destruction is a rational construct and it arises only after the capacity for reason has begun to develop, typically in late childhood and early adolescence. We must attempt to understand the idea of self-destruction in order to form a moral judgment of the act of self-destruction and we must analyze the idea in order to understand it. Our analysis will deliberately exclude any idea of self-destruction as it may be conceived by those who are mentally ill or by those whose mental faculties are immature or otherwise very poorly developed since such considerations are obviously beyond the scope of an intendedly rational investigation. Admittedly, the object of our analysis is highly complex and we may stand accused of sacrificing studied comprehensiveness for general clarity. Nonetheless, let us begin.

In all instances, those who conceive the idea of self-destruction attempt to terminate intense and unendurable personal suffering or the intense and unendurable suffering of other people within their social environment. The self-destroyers, whether actual or potential, will either be active or passive.

Those who are active are indignant or wrathful and they become assertive or aggressive. They intend either to dramatize social oppression or injustice through self-sacrificing protest or to destroy their enemies through self-sacrificing aggression.

We can refer to those who act to dramatize social oppression or injustice as heroic activists. If they hurt no one other than themselves, is it right that they should deliberately kill themselves in an attempt to bring about social change to end the unjust sufferings of others? The act is an act of heroism and, as such, it is purely subjective. It is a valid and noble personal decision to sacrifice oneself for a just cause that is greater than oneself, regardless of whether the act is immediately effective or not. Nonetheless, we must consider the act in context. In an oligarchy, there may be no alternative means to arouse popular support for a just cause; under democracy, there will be a number of effective ways to implement social change without requiring the suicide of the activist. Accordingly, we can approve of this extreme form of sociopolitical activism under oligarchy but not under democracy.

We must refer to those who act to destroy their enemies through self-sacrificing aggression as criminals since such persons either break the law by committing crime or take the law into their own hands by personally redressing their own injuries and/or losses resulting from crime. We can only condemn such suicides along with the murders with which they are usually directly associated.

The self-destroyers who are passive are extremely dejected, experiencing either overwhelming emotional pain or a combination of emotional and physical pain. Those who experience only emotional pain become emotionally debilitated, suffering either remorse or grief and acting both to punish themselves and to terminate their constant anguish. Feeling either intensely guilty or wholly deprived, they take steps to kill themselves, thereby putting an end to their misery but at the same time cheating themselves and permanently depriving others of themselves. Those who experience both emotional and physical pain usually suffer from terminal illness. They seek euthanasia to terminate their hopeless personal suffering.

We must refer to those who take steps to kill themselves because of their overwhelming personal grief or remorse as emotional cripples. Their suicides are condemnable on either of two grounds: one, that the self-destroyers have permanently deprived others of themselves (an issue of punishing the innocent), particularly where the self-destroyers have been caretakers and the ones who have relied upon such caretakers for their care can no longer rely upon them for that care and, two, that the self-destroyers have cheated themselves of the potential opportunity to overcome their private anguish and, once again or, perhaps, at long last, to experience genuine personal happiness (also an issue of punishing the innocent or, where this can not be said to be the case, of a self-imposed punishment that is overproportionate to the offense).

We will simply and plainly refer to those who seek euthanasia to terminate the pain of their terminal illnesses as the dying. To the extent that their illnesses are truly terminal, that their pain evidently can not be relieved through medication, and that cures for their illnesses unquestionably will not be forthcoming in time to save their lives, we can pass no moral judgment on their requests for euthanasia. Instead, we would do well to take up the cause of the dying, to relieve them of the necessity to request euthanasia, and to call for the standard practice of euthanasia throughout the medical profession in all cases of terminal illness where pain can not be relieved through medication and a cure is unknown or unavailable. Then euthanasia will no longer be an act of suicide and/or murder, but a responsible and caring act of the greatest compassion.

To conclude our analysis of the idea of self-destruction, we must restate our unequivocal condemnation both of the act of suicide and of the intention to commit suicide in all instances other than sociopolitical activism under oligarchy or euthanasia for the dying under specified conditions. The philosophy of symbiosism is generally unable to support the idea of self-destruction. On the issue of suicide, nature and reason are, for once, at one with each other. It is natural that we should favor life over death, Eros over Thanatos, creation over destruction, Vishnu over Shiva, and hope over despair. For nearly all of us, it is almost always more rational that we should will to live than to will to die. Only for one who is dying, whose insufferable pain can not otherwise be contained, may it sometimes be better to will to die than to wait to die. Only for one who is noble, exceptional, and extraordinary, may it sometimes be better to will to die than to will to live, when such a one wills, with supreme courage, to save or to improve the lives of others through heroic self-sacrifice without sacrificing the life of, or inflicting injury upon, any other person in the process.

As a final note, let us not fail to advocate moderation in the enjoyment of sensual pleasures, whether such enjoyment should be experienced in the form of eating, of ingesting mildly toxic substances (not for the nourishment but the stimulation or relaxation of the mind and body), or of engaging in sexual activity. The practice of moderation will produce beneficial consequences both in terms of preventing physical and emotional injury to oneself and, in the case of sexuality, of preventing emotional injury to others.

## 2. Humaneness

Humaneness is at the heart of the principle of noninjury. To be humane is to be considerate of, and compassionate towards, all other human beings and animals. If all human beings were to act humanely, both toward people and toward animals, injury, whether arising in recklessness or negligence or from deliberate malice, would decrease and care, the quintessential behavioral feature of all sentient and intelligent life, would increase.

The self-evident reason that we must practice noninjury is to reduce the intensity and the extent of human suffering. We have mentioned that we live in an age of advanced technology, a technology that is powerful, complex, useful, and highly beneficial but that is also, sometimes and in certain instances under particular circumstances, very dangerous, requiring of us all a new and higher level of responsibility toward others. We have also recognized that we have all arrived at once to a new self-consciousness in which we can see ourselves as members in common of a single species of life; therefore, the rational moral principle that protects the person and property of any one of us protects the persons and properties of all of us at all places in all times. It follows, then, that henceforth we must assume greater responsibility for ourselves and for others.

We have also advanced the idea, an idea that is revolutionary in our part of the world, in the West, indeed, in almost all of the world outside of certain parts of Asia, that we must extend our care, our sense of responsibility, our humaneness, to the lower species of animals. In Hinduism and Buddhism, the rationale for the practice of ahimsa is to protect the essence, or soul, of a living being, irrespective of the material form in which such an essence abides. According to the concept of samsara, any human being may have existed as an insect in a previous life, or may exist as an insect in a future life. The practical consequence of the practice of ahimsa, particularly in Buddhism, is to increase respect for human life within the context of an abiding reverence for all of life.

The intent of our rationale for extending the practice of noninjury to include the lower species of animals differs from the intent, but not the consequence, of ahimsa in Hinduism and Buddhism. Our rationale is twofold. First, to increase human awareness and acceptance of the general practice of noninjury among humankind, we would extend the practice to the lower species. This part of our rationale is not unlike that of an athlete who prepares for a five-mile race by training with a ten-mile run.

Both in its intent and consequence, the act of this part of our rationale is the same: to increase consideration and compassion for other human beings. The second part of our rationale is less self-serving. It is to protect the lower species of animals from needless and unjustified suffering at the hands of human beings. Whereas the humaneness of man with respect to man is at the heart of that which is most fundamental to beneficial reciprocity, the humaneness of man with respect to the lower species of animals is the direct and practicable expression of the magnanimity of mankind to the remainder of sentient life.

We have asked "Just how far down the phylogenetic tree must we descend to extend the practice of noninjury to all forms of sentient life?" In an attempt to offer a tentative response, let us suggest that to the extent to which it can be demonstrated that a member of a given species of animal life experiences pain when it has been injured, we must include its species among the species of the lower animals to which we extend the practice of noninjury. Such species will almost certainly include all of the mammals, probably all of the birds, and possibly all, or most, of the reptiles and the fishes. The proscription will almost certainly exclude the animals beneath the reptiles and the fishes on the phylogenetic tree since the brains and central nervous systems of the members of these species either are too primitive and inadequately developed to experience pain or are nonexistent. We must rely upon the science of biology to provide empirical data in support of a conclusive response to the question. Until then, we can infer a number of conclusive responses to related questions. "Should we become vegetarians?" Almost certainly, with respect to preventing the suffering of mammals by omitting meat from our diets; probably, with respect to omitting poultry; and possibly, with respect to omitting fish. "Should we no longer use fur in our wearing apparel?" Most certainly yes. "Should we give up hunting for sport?" Again, most certainly yes. "Should we give up fishing for sport as well?" Possibly yes but probably no: as with the question of whether to give up fish in our diets, we must wait until our knowledge of the degree of the experience of pain in fish is certain or only no more than slightly questionable.

We must attempt to provide an adequate response to one more question: "Will we be justified to grant a general exception to the broadest practicable extension of the principle of noninjury where the sacrifice of the lives or well-being of animals in medical research can save human lives or improve human well-being?" This question is the most difficult of all, because animals which have the most well-developed and advanced brains and central nervous systems (that is, those animals which are most like ourselves, such as the other primates) must be among the first species of animals to be spared our intentional injury; yet again, because they are the animals most like ourselves, they are generally the most valuable for medical research. Now, to the extent that animals can be used in medical experiments in which they experience no pain, we can offer little objection. Our concern arises only when we intentionally cause injury, or create a probable risk of injury, to innocent and helpless sentient beings. It is patently wrong to require the members of a lower species of animal life to suffer in the acquisition of knowledge for the exclusive or primary benefit of human beings. Such procedures of medical research comprise just one more form of specific imperialism. Accordingly, only a human being can serve as a subject in a medical experiment, and such a person must freely choose to serve as a subject. This kind of a decision is most certainly an act of magnanimity. At the present, medical science rightly must limit the number of subjects for its medical experiments to the number of heroic human volunteers who may be available. It remains our sincere hope and confident expectation that, in the not-too-distant future, the fruits of current advances in medical science and biotechnology will eliminate altogether any need to acquire living subjects for medical research.

## 3. Environmentalism

We have said that the moral principle of noninjury enjoins each person to refrain from injuring oneself, any other person, or any form of sentient or beneficial life (meaning by "beneficial life" any form of life that is necessary and beneficial for human life). What we have not yet talked about is that our concern not to injure not only is the concern not to injure directly but also the concern not to injure indirectly. Let us offer a few examples to clarify this distinction.

If a person shoots himself, he has directly injured himself; if, on the other hand, he abuses drugs and thereby, over time, causes irreparable damage to his liver, leading to his premature death, he has indirectly injured himself. If a person robs another person, he has directly injured that other person; if he calumniates another person, thereby effectively depriving that person of a substantial measure of professional and financial success, he has indirectly injured that other person. If a group of people removes a rain forest in order to provide land for industrial, commercial, and residential development, they have inflicted direct injury upon that rain forest; if they establish and maintain a nearby industry which generates substantial air pollution that causes continuous acid rain to fall upon the rain forest, they have inflicted indirect injury upon that rain forest. We have recognized that if the consequence of an unintentional act is equivalent to that of an intentional act, the unintentional act is just as blameworthy as the intentional act. Similarly, let us now establish that if the consequence of an indirect act is equivalent to that of a direct act, the indirect act is just as blameworthy as the direct act.

The causes of indirect injury are more subtle and less easily understood than those of direct injury even though, in the long run, the consequences of both forms of injury may be equally detrimental. With respect to self-preservation, the injunction not to injure oneself indirectly requires the moderation of sensuality. With respect to humaneness, the injunction only not unintentionally to injure any other person indirectly also requires, with respect to sexuality, the moderation of sensuality while the injunction not intentionally to injure any other person, or any form of sentient life, whether directly or indirectly, requires of every person the sublimation of aggression and of every society the legislation and enforcement of criminal law. With respect to environmentalism, the injunction not to injure, whether intentionally or unintentionally, any form of beneficial life, whether directly or indirectly, requires of every society the legislation and enforcement of environmental law. Let us now present a general theory of environmental law, the purpose of such a body of law must be to secure the permanent integrity of our biosphere.

Our biosphere consists of two essential parts: the inorganic natural environment (including the rocks, sediments, and soils of the continental crust of the earth; the rocks, basalt lavas, and muds of the oceanic crust; water, both fresh and saline; the atmosphere, or air; and sunlight) and the organic natural environment (including all of the species of life, both plants and animals).

The biosphere may be damaged either through the forces of nature (as by storms, earthquakes, volcanic eruptions, and the like) or through the use of modern technology by human beings (as by the burning of fossil fuels, the release of fluorocarbons into the atmosphere, the discharge of toxic wastes into the oceans, and the like). Natural damage to the biosphere typically generates an immediate temporary and particular detriment for certain species of life and, in time, a temporary and particular benefit for certain species; in general, the detriment suffered by certain individuals within a given species during a natural disaster appears to be counterbalanced by the benefit received by certain other individuals, whether of the same or of a different species. Let us cite but one example. Volcanic soils are known to be among the most fertile soils in the world and the natural habitats surrounding active volcanoes are among the most productive and diverse in nature, yet all life within the direct paths of the lava flows is destroyed during the immediate aftermath of a major volcanic eruption. Accordingly, our concern for the damage to our biosphere when caused by the forces of nature is essentially restricted to an interest in predicting the times and locations of the probable occurrences of such disasters so that the loss to human life and property, at best, can be avoided or, at worst, minimized. The problem of natural damage to the biosphere creates two valid policy issues for democratic government: generally effective natural catastrophe prediction and equitable compensation for economic loss. In considering these issues, however, we have been digressing and we must return now to the more relevant moral issue: the necessity that we ourselves refrain from inflicting substantial damage upon our own biosphere.

Air, soil, and water pollution control is the heart of environmental law. The origin of environmental pollution can be attributed to the widespread and uncontrolled use, misuse, and abuse of modern technology by large populations for the satisfaction of basic human needs and desires. Environmental pollution has become a pervasive modern problem, having arisen rather abruptly as a function of the conjunction and interaction of accelerating increases in human population and unprecedented advances in industrial technology. There are several categories of technological abuse: the consumption of fuel to create energy for communication, transportation, and industry; the use of various toxic chemicals in certain products (as in fertilizers, pesticides, defoliants, detergents, lubricants, refrigerants, and electrical equipment) and modes of application (including solids, dusts, aerosols, gases, sprays, solvents, and liquids); the ineffective disposal of industrial and commercial wastes as well as the general wastes of consumers (including sewage, garbage, and rubbish); and thermal pollution (wherein industrial wastewaters are discharged into natural waters at very high, or very low, temperatures, thereby killing or injuring organisms in their natural habitats). All of these technological abuses are highly detrimental to mankind, either directly, by injuring, or threatening to injure, the health and well-being of the people living at the vulnerable locations, or indirectly, by injuring, or threatening to injure, the biosphere upon which the health and well-being of all people are dependent. Accordingly, effective air, soil, and water pollution control is an essential and inescapable policy issue for all democratic governments.

There are a number of measures which democratic governments employ, or can employ, to implement effective pollution control. With respect to industrial waste, government can require that industry install and operate pollution control equipment, offering tax credits as a positive incentive while revoking or denying a license to operate as a negative incentive where a business is either unwilling or unable to introduce the required equipment. In the latter case, government must assist workers of shut down companies to make an economic transition to other companies within the same industry, or to companies in different industries, which do not pollute the environment or do not fail to control their pollution in an effective manner. With respect to consumer waste, government can regulate public waste dumps and sanitary landfills, requiring that specific techniques be employed for the safe disposal of hazardous and toxic substances. Government can regulate both the operation and the manufacture of air-polluting vehicles through vehicle registration and by establishing, monitoring, and enforcing rigid emission control standards. No operators, then, would be permitted to drive, and no manufacturers, to sell, any vehicles which would fail to meet these standards.

Flora and fauna conservation is the third area of environmental law that imposes an absolute obligation upon democratic government. Unlike antipollution, which protects the biosphere from indirect injury caused by the use, misuse, and abuse of human technology, conservation protects the biosphere, including all of the nonhuman living things, from direct injury, both unintentional and otherwise, inflicted by man. Conservation is something like the idea of the biblical myth of Noah's Ark, where a sufficient number of individuals from each species to ensure reproduction is saved from annihilation to rejuvenate and to repopulate the earth following the catastrophic deluge. The science of ecology will undoubtedly inform us in due time just how many green plants we must maintain to provide an adequate supply of oxygen in the atmosphere, just which species of plants and animals we must preserve to provide an adequate source of medicines for the maintenance of optimal health (both physical and mental) in human beings, and just which among the biological categories of living things are most useful, if not indispensable, in maintaining the balance of nature and in preventing or controlling future outbreaks of drought, famine, and disease. Until then, we would do well to conserve that which we still have, both of plants and animals.

There are three unequivocal measures by which government can implement effective conservation: by maintaining zoos and botanical gardens in urban centers as well as a system of wildlife reservations, parks, and sanctuaries in rural and wilderness areas; by prohibiting or restricting the killing or capture of endangered species; and by prohibiting or restricting the destruction of natural habitats in the development of privately-owned lands. The implementation and enforcement of these measures will permit man to exercise his new role as steward of the biosphere. Through the effective and universal establishment and enforcement of environmental law (particularly once mankind has come together to form a single political entity, a world democratic federal government), human beings will become fully responsible for, as they continue to be fully dependent upon, all , or most, of the nonhuman species of life, while at the same time, all, or most, of the nonhuman species will become fully dependent upon, and, in a very real sense, fully responsible for, the enduring happiness and well-being of all human beings.

# II.
# The Second Principle of Ethics—Utility

The rationale for the principle of utility is so simple as to be self-evident. We do the things which enable us to satisfy the needs of life or to eliminate its sufferings. The things that we do either will achieve this end or serve as a means to achieve it. Such activity, then, is "useful."

All activities which are useful are good, and all such activities must at least be tolerated, if not actively encouraged, regardless of whether certain activities should appear to be "more useful" than others. To see why this should be so, we must consider two examples.

Out of one hundred people who profess to enjoy listening to classical music, as many as, say, ninety may profess to enjoy listening to Mozart's Thirty-ninth Symphony while as few as ten may profess to enjoy listening to Bach's Three Sonatas for Unaccompanied Violin. Are these esoteric Bach compositions "less useful" than this particular Mozart symphony? No, because the Bach pieces may have the greater utility for certain lovers of classical music, most probably for advanced students of the violin and quite possibly for students of musical composition.

Out of one hundred people who have experienced some level of education, three hold doctoral degrees as their highest level of educational achievement; thirteen, masters degrees; forty, bachelors degrees; forty-two, high school diplomas; while two stopped attending school after completing eighth grade. In terms of cumulative educational experience, we can say that one hundred completed eighth grade; ninety-eight, high school; fifty-six, a college or university undergraduate program; sixteen, a university graduate program; and three, a doctoral program. Yet, no one can say that the doctoral program is "less useful" than an eighth grade education because the doctoral program provided a benefit for the least number while the eighth grade education provided a benefit for the greatest number.

We should be able to see that any useful act will always be generally useful, meaning that it will be useful for "the greatest number," that is, for society as a whole, although it may, or it may not, be particularly useful for any single person at any given time. Thus, "education" is "useful" because, in general, it advances human knowledge and, in particular, at one time or another, it prepares each person to engage in a useful occupation. "Work" is "useful" because it provides the wherewithal to satisfy the necessities of life. Both "entertainment" and "recreation" are "useful" because they allow people to rest from work and to divert their attention from the demands and stresses of work. "Medical care" is "useful" because it relieves pain, prevents or cures disease, and helps to restore and to maintain a healthy body and a sound mind. "Eating" is "useful" because it nourishes the body. "Sleep" is "useful" because it restores strength and promotes healing. "Sexual intercourse" is "useful" because it enables us to procreate. At the most rudimentary level, nature has motivated us to satisfy our physiological needs by providing an increasing sensual discomfort during the onset and subsequent course of the sensation of a need and a countervailing intense sensual pleasure during the course of its satisfaction.

The greatest value of the principle of utility lies in its singular effectuality to rank and to prioritize the acts of utility. While it will always remain true that all activities which are useful are good, it is patently undeniable that popular opinion is generally multifarious and constantly changeable. If, at any given time, the majority of people prefer drinking orange juice to eating applesauce, we can rely upon the principle of supply and demand operating under a system of free-fair capitalism to assure that the number of orange groves will exceed that of apple orchards. If, at a later time, the converse should become true, the same system of capitalism will serve to create an adequate supply to meet the change in demand. Since all activities which are useful are good, it really does not matter whether farmers grow oranges or apples; it only matters that they respond to, and provide for, the immediate nutritional needs and desires of people.

In recognition that useful activity must bring into balance the satisfaction of the needs of the one and the many, let us conclude our discussion of the useful by affirming that useful activity must include not only that which satisfies the changing needs and tastes of the common majority, but that which satisfies both the basic needs (but possibly unusual tastes) of atypical minorities and the highest, most complex, and unique

needs and tastes of any one of us, which must needs be include the esoteric needs of the most extraordinary and gifted persons among us, subject only to the constraints of the marketplace. Accordingly, the optimal
mix and extent of useful activity will be present in those societies which
are open, free, and just, which is to say, in modern democratic societies.

Having considered useful activity, we must examine the two remaining kinds of human behavior, which include both useless and abusive
activities. Let us begin with the latter.

Human activity is abusive when a person misuses his or her abilities
to work with tools and machinery and/or to guide and to influence other
people with the consequence that he or she inflicts injury upon at least
one other person. Obviously, any effort to prevent or to correct abusive
behavior initially must fall within the province of the principle of noninjury. If, however, any person fails to refrain from harming others, either
by not resolving not to harm others or by not taking steps to avoid such
situations and circumstances in which one might unintentionally or acci-
dentally come to cause harm to others, then any effort to control or to
change abusive behavior quite properly falls within the province of the
principle of utility, where a person, or a group of people, engage in useful activity for the purpose of preventing or minimizing a detriment to
the greatest number. This area of human activity includes the professions
and occupations of medicine, law, and social work in addition to the
most fundamental operations of democratic government. The effort also
occasionally falls within the province of the principle of magnanimity, as
when a person acts either as a hero to rescue (or to shield) other persons
from the consequences of human misconduct or as a humanitarian to alleviate the sufferings of the victims of abuse, when the injury caused or
threatened by abusive behavior is not, can not be, or will not be, re-
dressed through the normal operation of the law.

Human activity which does not enable us to satisfy the needs of life
or to eliminate or to reduce our sufferings, even though otherwise such
activity does not inflict injury upon others, is useless activity. An activity
that is deemed to be useless may further be deemed to be wasteful, since
few will fail to observe that the time that has been lost during vain pur-
suits may have been better spent in worthwhile endeavors. As with the
evaluations of useful and abusive activities, the evaluation of useless activity may seem to be highly subjective. Actually, it is not; rather, it is
highly relative, because the objective determination of that which is useful, or useless, or even abusive, largely depends upon the particular period in the life of a person or the particular stage in the development of a
society. To arrive at a valid evaluation of usefulness, abusiveness, or use-

lessness, we first need to have a reasonably accurate assessment of general human needs and hurts. We should ultimately be able to rely upon the science of psychology to provide us this information with a reasonable degree of certainty. At the present, the hierarchy of needs model advanced by Abraham Maslow appears, in my opinion, to provide an excellent point of departure.

David Hume once said that "Reason is, and ought only to be, the slave of passions." In part, I disagree with this assertion. In my earliest book, *The Values*, I offered a different conclusion with respect to the interrelationships between the fundamental divisions and functions of the human mind. I posited that since the will is that part of the mind that moves man to action, it is the most important part of the mind. The will is composed of three basic parts. The part which is the most primitive and which has the longest genetic history is the part which responds to physiological needs and hurts: it directs primary action, including all of our natural urges and reflexes and the habits which we have developed to accommodate their satisfaction or healing. The part which is a little less primitive and which has a genetic history which is not quite as old is the complex of emotions, which is to say, the complex of conscious reflections upon the sensations of pain or pleasure: it directs secondary action, including all of our emotional reactions to sensory stimuli. The part which is most advanced and which has a genetic history approximately equivalent to the history of the zoological family Hominidae is the part which conceptualizes, that is, it includes and it makes use of reason: it directs tertiary action, including all of our voluntary behavior that follows a predetermined course of action and adheres to a given program of values. Accordingly, rather than concur with Hume's dictum that "Reason is . . . the slave of passions," I would counterargue that reason is always only in the service of happiness. Utility, then, is in the service of satisfying human needs and of alleviating human suffering.

There are four kinds of "useless" activity. We will discuss them now, beginning with that that is most easy to understand.

The first is rest, when one enjoys freedom from activity or labor to restore one's vitality and equanimity. The various categories of rest include sleep, recreation, entertainment, shopping, visiting with friends, eating, napping, and the like. Obviously, this kind of "useless" activity serves an undeniably useful purpose: to restore the mental and physical energies of the worker so that he or she can resume productive activity. Rest becomes morally objectionable only if it is inordinately prolonged, so that one intentionally consumes more than one produces, or gives an impression of attempting to produce.

The second kind comprises activity which, in the present, appears to be useless but which, eventually, both will be evidently and directly useful. Examples of this kind of activity include the systematic pursuit of knowledge through the application of the scientific method or the efforts of research and development departments in modern business corporations to design and to improve consumer products and the manufacturing processes by which such products are created. With this kind of activity, there will be many failures in advance of each success but without this kind of activity, there can be little or no success.

The third kind of "useless" activity is that kind of activity which is always apparently useless but which is, at the same time, actually useful, but in an indirect manner. We are not talking here about useful activity that serves as a means to an end, such as a course in mathematics during a person's education. We are talking about artistic creativity. We are addressing the problem of aesthetics under the principle of utility. We are reexamining the traditional dichotomy between utility and beauty. If we can succeed in arguing that beauty, artistic as well as natural, is beneficial (if not essential) for human well-being, then we can conclude that artistic creativity is never useless activity.

Beauty, whether natural or artistic, is a perception of objects and/or the effects of energies upon objects, whether in space or time, or both space and time, which are formed in such a way as to serve as a symbol of the satisfaction of need or of attaining security from harm, or of some value held by the perceiver which provides a systematic plan for the satisfaction of need or for attaining security from harm, and which causes a temporary sensation of pleasure and a temporary emotion of happiness. Beauty, then, is symbolic of the fulfillment of need or the deliverance from harm. It is not an actual fulfillment or deliverance but a vicarious experience of the same. For as long as we live, we will experience recurring needs to be satisfied and hurts to be avoided, prevented, or alleviated. Since we will always experience needs and hurts, and since it will also be impossible for us not to be able to experience beauty whenever we experience needs and hurts, it follows that we will always experience beauty. Therefore, the question before us is not whether we will experience beauty but whether our experience of beauty is beneficial or detrimental. We would submit that it is always beneficial. The satisfaction of needs and the mitigation of hurts generally cause a sensation of pleasure and an emotion of happiness. Both the sensation and the emotion quickly dissipate, first the sensation, then the emotion. A renewal of pleasure and happiness will not occur until the next times that needs are satisfied and hurts are mitigated. However, the experience of beauty also causes a sen-

sation of pleasure and an emotion of happiness, generally at times in between the times when the satisfaction of needs and the mitigation of hurts
cause pleasure and happiness. Also, while the experience of beauty does
not directly facilitate our efforts to satisfy our needs and to mitigate our
hurts, neither does it hinder them. We must conclude, then, that the experience of beauty generally increases human pleasure and happiness and
that, accordingly, beauty is beneficial for human well-being.

The fourth kind of "useless" activity is that kind of activity which is
always apparently useful. albeit in an indirect manner, but which is, at
the same time, actually useless, and not only actually useless, but sometimes actually abusive. We are talking now about religious practice.
Now, some may argue that religion, like beauty, increases human pleasure and happiness since it creates a sense of peace and security. However, since we can neither prove that God exists nor does not exist, we
can not be certain that our religious practice does not proceed out of a
simple form of self-deception. If it does, it might still be considered
completely harmless were it not for three insuperable problems which
require that we abandon and ignore religious practice, sooner or later and
for the rest of time, regardless of its form or tradition.

The first problem is the problem of religious warfare. Lasting world
peace and an immediate improvement in human well-being require that
mankind unite under one world sovereignty and that all warfare, regardless of its cause, be prohibited and eliminated. Therefore, any religion
which advocates warfare, strife, or militancy of any kind can no longer
be tolerated and must be denounced and renounced.

The second problem is the problem of religious ethics. The moral
foundation of a unified world must be predicted upon the one quality that
is distinctive of, and common to, all human beings—reason—and not
upon the combined ethical traditions of multifarious and widely conflic-
tive religions. Therefore, only that among the combined body of religious
ethics which is useful for, and conducive to, universal human well-being
must be retained, with the remainder discarded, and all that which is retained must then be morally translated from the language of ancient
dogmatic proclamation to that of modern rational expression.

The third problem is the problem of insecurity that proceeds from
our total, or even primary, reliance upon the goodness and power of a
supreme being the very existence of which is, at best, not quite certain
and, at worst, highly doubtful. We must neither be able to blame others
nor God for our personal moral irresponsibility. The moral foundation of
a unified world must be stronger than any religious morality. It must be
stronger than Jewish, Hindu, or Islamic morality. It must be stronger than

Christian or Buddhist morality. It must be the strongest morality that mankind has ever known because it is the only morality that is fully predicated upon reason. In the absence of a sudden universal revelation by a supreme being, religion either will eventually become obsolete or it will evolve into something completely new. Its undue persistence will impose an opportunity cost upon every person and impair the cohesion of the universal society. For so long as people are able to lose themselves in fantasy, they will refuse to acknowledge the reality of the human condition. So long as people believe that the course of their lives is dependent upon their acceptance or rejection of divine providence, they will fail to assume full responsibility for their own actions. They will be unable to have complete faith in themselves since their faith is centered in something outside of themselves. Notwithstanding this problem of insecurity, or ambiguity, which creates such a great moral dilemma for human beings in the modern world, we must remain tolerant of religious practice and we would do well not to oppose it unless it is overtly hostile or abusive to nonbelievers. We must maintain this position for two reasons. First, our opposition, although grounded in reason, may only create a greater harm than the harm that we are attempting to do away with. We can no sooner correct the errors of religion through rational argument than force a student of mathematics to master calculus or trigonometry when he or she is unable or unwilling to learn algebra or geometry. Second, the functions of religion may evolve over time to emphasize ethics and sociability and to de-emphasize theism and divine worship. If religion endures, it will most likely transform into something entirely different from what it is at the present or has ever been in the past. Therefore, although it is essentially useless and potentially wasteful for and abusive to its own followers, we must continue to tolerate religion, thereby upholding the freedom of individuals and groups to seek truth in their own ways and on their own terms without interference. But if religion remains essentially useless and becomes increasingly dangerous and abusive so that we should do best to repudiate it altogether, what will remain that we might be able to believe in? What can we believe in that will never become obsolete for as long as the human species endures? What can we believe in that will always be neither irrational nor inhuman? We will be able to believe that all truth that is relevant to human happiness is ultimately knowable. This is, and will continue to be, the only proper object of faith. This must become the ultimate and supreme faith of the human species.

# III.
# Utilitarianism

Utilitarianism is the moral philosophy that is determined according to the criterion of the principle of utility. It originated independently in ancient Chinese philosophy and in ancient Greek philosophy.

Utilitarianism was first seen in the philosophy of Mo Tzu (about 470 – 391 B.C.), who was born about ten years after the death of Confucius and who lived at about the same time as Socrates. Confucius had introduced the principle of *jen*, or love between human beings, but the concept, as it came to be understood in the subsequent development and practice of his teachings, emphasized the unique love, reciprocity, and loyalty between persons within five particular social relationships (sovereign and subject, father and son, husband and wife, brother and brother, and friend and friend). Mo Tzu, on the other hand, advocated universal love without predetermined preferences. His fundamental concern was for the general well-being of the common people and he affirmed only that kind of behavior and activity which might provide for the physical security and the material needs of all people. He advocated activity that is beneficial and that corrects, prevents, or avoids activity that is harmful. It is intriguing today to recognize that the roots of utilitarianism were planted in the Far East almost twenty-five hundred years ago. It is regrettable, although understandable, that since Mo Tzu's vision of *jen* de-emphasized the preferential love associated with given social positions and since he deemed as wasteful the cultivation of the fine arts, the observance of ceremony, and attention to decorum, his philosophy failed to flourish, or even to remain active, throughout most of the lengthy history of imperial China.

Utilitarianism was next seen at Athens about one hundred years later in the philosophy of Epicurus (341 – 270 B.C.). For Epicurus, pleasure and pain comprise the cardinal criteria for the determination of right conduct. The experience of pleasure and pain includes not only physiological sensations but emotional reactions and conditions, such as equanimity (that is, peace of mind, or that to which the ancient Greek philosophers referred by the term *ataraxia*), happiness, or delight, and anxiety, fear, and anger. To attain pleasure and to avoid pain, one must recognize that the satisfaction of one's essential needs is usually not very difficult to accomplish since these needs are generally few and simple. Therefore, one must diligently reject or patiently overcome all of one's needless desires and aspirations; one would do best as early as possible not to entertain false hopes and illusions. Whatever activity or behavior enables one to satisfy one's essential needs is useful; all other activity or behavior is wasteful or harmful. It is highly noteworthy that the roots of utilitarianism should have been planted in the West at almost the same time, albeit unrelatedly, that they had in the East. It is also highly regrettable that Epicureanism, like Moism, should have flourished only for some four or five centuries before entering into a total eclipse.

Fifteen hundred years or so would elapse before utilitarianism would reemerge, this time appearing in Great Britain in its modern form as introduced by Jeremy Bentham (*The Principles of Morals and Legislation*, 1781) and further developed by his principal follower, John Stuart Mill (*Utilitarianism*, 1863).

Utilitarianism is grounded in the principles of the science of psychology. It is axiomatic in psychology that an organism experiences the sensation of tension, uneasiness, or discomfort upon the onset of a physiological need, such as hunger, thirst, sexual desire, or fatigue, and a sensation of pleasure when the need has been satisfied, as through eating, drinking, sexual intercourse, or sleep. Likewise, an organism experiences the sensation of pain when it suffers an illness or an injury, and a sensation of relief from such pain that is temporary when effective medical treatment has been received, often with the administration of an appropriate analgesic, and permanent, or what we would think of as the usual, normal, and neutral sensation that is indicative of wellness, when the illness has been cured or the injury healed. Discomfort or pain, then, serves as a signal to the organism that there is a need to be satisfied or a hurt to be healed; pleasure or painlessness, that a need is being, or has recently been, satisfied or a hurt healed. Accordingly, pleasure and pain are necessary for survival. Utilitarianism enables human beings to determine which plans and acts are optimal for the satisfaction of needs and the elimination or mitigation of hurts.

It should somewhat improve our own understanding of utilitarianism if we would pause to consider Bentham's own conception of it. In chapter one, "On the Principle of Utility" from *The Principles of Morals and Legislation*, (a very brief portion of which we have previously quoted and for the redundancy of which within the present context we request the reader's acquiescence), Bentham writes:

Nature has placed mankind under the governance of two sovereign masters, pain and pleasure. It is for them alone to point out what we ought to do, as well as to determine what we shall do. On the one hand the standard of right and wrong, on the other the chain of causes and effects, are fastened to their throne. They govern us in all we do, in all we say, in all we think: every effort we can make to throw off our subjection, will serve but to demonstrate and confirm it. In words a man may pretend to abjure their empire: but in reality he will remain subject to it all the while. The principle of utility recognizes this subjection, and assumes it for the foundation of that system, the object of which is to rear the fabric of felicity by the hands of reason and of law. Systems which attempt to question it, deal in sounds instead of sense, in caprice instead of reason, in darkness instead of light.

But enough of metaphor and declamation: it is not by such means that moral science is to be improved.

The principle of utility is the foundation of the present work: it will be proper therefore at the outset to give an explicit and determinate account of what is meant by it. By the principle of utility is meant that principle which approves or disapproves of every action whatsoever, according to the tendency which it appears to have to augment or diminish the happiness of the party whose interest is in question: or, what is the same thing in other words, to promote or to oppose that happiness. I say of every action whatsoever; and therefore not only of every action of a private individual, but of every measure of government.

By utility is meant that property in any object, whereby it tends to produce benefit, advantage, pleasure, good, or happiness (all this in the present case comes to the same thing) or (what comes again to the same thing) to prevent the happening of mischief, pain, evil, or unhappiness to the party whose interest is considered: if that party be the community in general, then the happiness of the community: if a particular individual, then the happiness of that individual.

The interest of the community is one of the most general expressions that can occur in the phraseology of morals: no wonder that the meaning of it is often lost. When it has a meaning, it is this. The community is a fictitious body, composed of the individual persons who are considered as constituting as it were its members. The interest of the community then is, what?—the sum of the interests of the several members who compose it.

It is in vain to talk of the interest of the community, without understanding what is the interest of the individual. A thing is said to promote the interest, or to be for the interest, of an individual, when it tends to add to the sum total of his pleasures: or, what comes to the same thing, to diminish the sum total of his pains.

An action then may be said to be conformable to the principle of utility, or, for shortness sake, to utility, (meaning with respect to the community at large) when the tendency it has to augment the happiness of the community is greater than any it has to diminish it.

A measure of government (which is but a particular kind of action, performed by a particular person or persons) may be said to be conformable to or dictated by the principle of utility, when in like manner the tendency which it has to augment the happiness of the community is greater than any which it has to diminish it.

When an action, or in particular a measure of government, is supposed by a man to be conformable to the principle of utility, it may be convenient, for the purposes of discourse, to imagine a kind of law or dictate, called a law or dictate of utility: and to speak of the action in question, as being conformable to such law or dictate.

A man may be said to be a partizan of the principle of utility, when the approbation or disapprobation he annexes to any action, or to any measure, is determined by and proportioned to the tendency which he conceives it to have to augment or to diminish the happiness of the community: or in other words, to its conformity or unconformity to the laws or dictates of utility.

Of an action that is conformable to the principle of utility one may always say either that it is one that ought to be done, or at least that it is not one that ought not to be done. One may say also, that it is right it should be done; at least that it is not wrong it should be done: that it is a right action; at least that it is not a wrong action. When thus interpreted, the words *ought*, and *right* and *wrong*, and others of that stamp, have a meaning: when otherwise, they have none.

In this manner, the fundamental principles of utilitarianism are set forth in the first four pages of the great book. While both Bentham and Mill maintain that utilitarianism is applicable at once to the actions of individuals and groups, we would argue that utilitarianism is primarily a social ethics, one that applies to the actions of individuals only to the extent that they affect the well-being of individuals beyond the practitioner's personal circle, that is, the well-being of the community or of society. This means, of course, that no one is ever at liberty to injure or to threaten anyone else; it does mean, however, that any person is always free to favor, or not to favor, or to withdraw favor from, or to restore favor to, particular other persons in the usual course of his or her private actions.

Utilitarianism is highly objective. Its achievements (or the activities of human beings that are implemented according to the principles of utilitarianism) can be evaluated through quantitative and qualitative measures. Utilitarianism is most appropriate to function as a social ethics. Its principles can be applied to determine optimal courses and degrees of social action, especially with respect to corporate, institutional, and governmental activity. It can enable a society to distinguish clearly between beneficial and detrimental behaviors and activities. Its principles can be relied upon to create lasting justice and security in society through the formulation (or reformulation), administration, and adjudication of a meaningful and effective body of incontrovertible laws.

Utilitarianism has given birth to two complementary and practical ideologies. Its principles are applied very easily and effectively in either of these ideologies. One is a political ideology, the only political ideology that has rational and demonstrable validity, the ideology of democracy. Democracy is concerned with creating and sustaining that kind of government in which the greatest number can participate and which will provide protections that are adequate and reliable, and services that are beneficial and not otherwise easily available, if available at all, for the greatest number. The other is an economic ideology, the only economic ideology that has rational and demonstrable validity, the ideology of capitalism, specifically free-fair capitalism (that is, mixed capitalism or regulated capitalism), the form of capitalism that is currently practiced in the great democracies of the world. Capitalism is concerned with creating and sustaining that kind of economy in which the greatest number can participate and which will enable the creation and distribution of goods and services to supply the needs of the greatest number. Let us now examine more closely how each of these ideologies, as the practical applications of the social ethics of utilitarianism, can function effectively to accomplish lasting peace and prosperity in a unified world. Inasmuch as politics precedes economics, let us begin with a discussion of democracy.

Democracy is that form of government in which sovereignty is accorded by the people to themselves and exercised by the people directly, where feasible (as in very small societies), or indirectly through a system of representation as determined in regular and frequent elections, where the direct exercise of sovereignty is infeasible (as in almost all modern societies except the very smallest). Democracy, then, is the best form of government for accessing knowledge of the continuous distresses, difficulties, needs, desires, and hopes of the greatest number of people within any given society. Only that form of government which is most able to access such critical popular information will be able to provide an apposite benefit or relief for the greatest number. Accordingly, democracy is the only consistent political expression of utilitarianism.

Under democracy, society accords sovereignty to its entire membership by means of the social contract. The social contract is an agreement between the members of society that defines and limits the rights and obligations of each person and of society as that entity that is identical to, and that faithfully represents, the unity and the collective interests of all persons, in other words, of every citizen and the government.

The social contract is expressed by means of a constitution, which is a written instrument incorporating the fundamental principles and laws of a nation or other sovereign territory. The social contract is generally written in behalf of the people by the appointed representatives of the people, or by agents appointed by those representatives, and it is subsequently ratified by the people through the agency of their representatives.

The first true social contract in the history of mankind, the Constitution of the United States of America, was drafted by the appointed representatives of the American people in 1787. The preamble to the Constitution is a succinct expression of the social contract. It reads: "We the people of the United States, in order to form a more perfect union, establish justice, insure domestic tranquillity, provide for the common defence, promote the general welfare, and secure the blessings of liberty to ourselves and our posterity, do ordain and establish this constitution for the United States of America." The text of the Constitution then follows, comprising the various articles and amendments, which express in detail the rights and obligations of the state and its citizens.

The complete social contract embraces the entire law of the land, although the national constitution and, ultimately, the supranational constitution and/or the world constitution, remain the cardinal elements within it. The complete social contract must comprise the aggregate of the federal constitution and the constitutions of each of the constituent governments within the federation at each of the levels of government for the jurisdictions wherein the citizens reside. It must also comprise the aggregate of all laws, statutes, and ordinances from all levels of government.

The social contract establishes the fundamental laws to satisfy the requirements of security and justice in a functional democratic society. These requirements fall into two categories: those which provide justice throughout society while instituting the form and apparatus of democratic government, and those which protect personal freedoms while ensuring intellectual integrity. The fair requirements of democratic government generate principles and measures which must be introduced to ensure that democracy will work effectively for the benefit of all of the members of society. Foremost among these principles is the quintessential utilitarian political principle, the principle of universal suffrage. This principle ensures that each mature person (which is to say, each person who has reached the age of majority or, in other words, has become an adult) will always have an equal opportunity to participate in the formulation and execution of the decisions, policies, and activities of his or her government. Other principles and related measures include those which are necessary to establish and to sustain the practice of majority rule and an effective diffusion of political authority. On the other hand, the free requirements of democratic government generate principles and measures which must be introduced or sanctioned to establish and to sustain such safeguards and enabling practices as freedom of conscience, religious freedom, religious toleration, separation of church and state, separation of religion and politics, free access to relevant information, academic freedom, freedom of speech, freedom of the press, an informed citizenry, public debate of political issues, the party system, and protection of individual and minority rights.

To prevent the usurpation of power when democratic government is entrusted to and administered by elected officials and appointed representatives, the structure and apparatus of government must provide an effective diffusion of political authority such that neither all of the executive, legislative, and judicial functions of government nor even any combination of two of the three functions is not accorded to a single office or official. This principle has become known as the separation of powers and, with respect to the separation of the executive and legislative functions of government, was advocated by Locke in the second of the *Two Treatises of Government* (1690) while, with respect to the separation of all three functions, was advocated by Montesquieu in *The Spirit of the Laws* (1748). Upon the federal union of the thirteen British colonies of North America into a single, new, and autonomous democratic nation in 1789, a new kind of diffusion of political authority came into being, one in which the executive, legislative, and judicial functions of government not only were separated but were distributed as evenly as practicable between the various levels of government (namely, the national or federal government, the state or provincial government, and the local government, whether county, township, or municipality). After considerable deliberation and controversy, the founders of the American government rejected both the unitary and confederate forms of government in favor of a new form, the federation, which created an intermediate position between the unitary and confederate forms. The argument for the principles of federalism, principles which were incorporated into the United States Constitution, was essentially the collective creative effort of three Americans:    Alexander Hamilton, James Madison, and John Jay, who wrote a series of eight-five essays to present and to advance the argument to the American people. The essays were published both serially in New York City newspapers (1787-1788) and as a book (1789). The essays, known as *The Federalist*, comprise a brilliant and effective argument for the multidimensional diffusion of political authority in a democratic government.

The principle of the diffusion of political authority is crucial to prevent a democracy from regressing into an oligarchy. With the separation of the powers of the three branches of government on each of the horizontal levels of a federal democracy and the distribution of the responsibilities and operations of government between the several vertical levels, an extensive and highly effective multidirectional, or crosshatch, diffusion of political authority can be established and sustained to ensure that the powers of democratic government are always used in the service, and for the benefit, of all of the people.

In a previous book, *Toward World Sovereignty*, I have attempted to present an argument and a methodology for the creation of a world democratic federal government. The recent progress of the human species requires that we leap to accomplish this change in the sovereignty and the political organization of the nations of the world without delay. If we fail in this effort, we will fail not only to maintain the impetus of our current progress but most likely even to survive as a species, or otherwise to prevent or to avoid the annihilation of a substantial portion of our species, due to the consequences of nuclear, chemical, and/or biological warfare.

To create world unity, we will certainly require an objective basis for a common morality:    we will need to establish universal law. Universal law must be identified with the universal social contract. It must comprise the constitution of the universal democratic federation and the combined constitutions, statutory laws, and secondary legislation of all of the member nations and territories. We will consider the binding elements of universal law in detail in the next chapter. First, however, we must complete our presentation of utilitarianism with a discussion of free-fair capitalism.

We have said that capitalism "is concerned with creating and sustaining that kind of economy in which the greatest number can participate and which will enable the creation and distribution of goods and services to supply the needs of the greatest number." Some will say that this is the concern of socialism as well, or even that this is not at all the concern of capitalism but only of socialism. We would reply by saying that while the greatest number can participate in a socialist economy, a socialist economy will not enable the creation and distribution of goods and services to supply the needs of the greatest number. This is so because a socialist economy can only be administered by an oligarchical government and the leaders of an oligarchical government are solely, or primarily, interested in providing benefits, or the greatest share of benefits, for the members of their own class. Even if this were not so, and a socialist economy of sorts were to be administered by a democratic government, those persons elected or appointed to plan and to manage the economy, no matter how gifted or experienced, could never accurately identify and effectively supply the needs of the greatest number. (Now, by way of a personal example, no one else, except perhaps those who are closest to me, can surely know what comprises all of my personal needs, just as I can not surely know what comprises all of the personal needs of anyone else. Another person may know that I must eat, but he or she may not know what I like to eat. I may reason that some other person, a person whom I have never met nor have even ever seen, must wear clothes but I do not know what kind of clothes that person likes to wear.) Therefore, socialism can not provide an effective economic application of utilitarianism.

Capitalism, on the other hand, postulates private ownership and utilization of capital. The foremost requirement of capitalism is individual freedom. If each person in society is free to do whatever he or she does best and, for the primary sake of one's personal economic gain, to learn to identify and to supply the needs of other people, then everyone, or almost everyone, will benefit and prosper in a way that is not possible under any other kind of economy.

Even under capitalism, experience has demonstrated that the markets can not always be relied upon to react to the forces of supply and demand in such a manner as to create and to distribute all of the goods and services necessary to supply the needs of the greatest number. This is so for two reasons.

First, the forces of nature may interfere with economic prosperity, as when natural disasters occur, such as droughts, floods, earthquakes, volcanic eruptions, and the like. Second, human nature is such that people sometimes react to economic phenomena in a manner that is more emotional than rational, as when people, seeing that stock prices are beginning to fall, imagine the approach of an economic downturn and sell all of their personal holdings in a panic reaction, thereby precipitating further declines in stock prices and creating a self-fulfilling prophesy. To overcome these and certain other kinds of problems, such as monopoly, or what we might think of as economic oligarchy, democratic government has introduced a modest degree of economic regulation, thereby transforming traditional laissez-faire capitalism into mixed capitalism, or what I would call, by virtue of its consequences for society, free-fair capitalism, meaning a kind of capitalism that provides the optimal balance or mix of personal economic freedom and social economic justice for all of the members of society. This economic regulation is accomplished not only by maintaining and supervising an adequate money supply and banking system but by implementing monetary policy and fiscal policy as advanced by the English economist John Maynard Keynes in his magnum opus *The General Theory of Employment, Interest, and Money* (1936). We need not review the details of the theory and practice of free-fair capitalism at this time since this information is widely known through modern economic science and can be readily accessed from other sources. We will only comment that the efficacy of free-fair capitalism has been tested in the United States and the United Kingdom for more than seventy years and that the results of this testing over this initial and admittedly somewhat limited span appear to demonstrate that free-fair capitalism is generally effective in achieving the practical economic objectives of utilitarianism.

As soon as the world can be unified under a universal democratic federal government, the practical applications of utilitarianism will become available and operable throughout the earth in both government at every level and in all of the markets of the global economy to accomplish six objectives which will provide permanent security and an immediate improvement in the quality of life for all of the world's people. The six objectives include:  one, the universal security and total preservation of the human species, and of all species of life on the earth, through the writing, interpretation, and enforcement of binding universal law with the immediate and irrevocable criminalization of war; two, the permanent increase in the local security of each person and his or her property by means of national disarmament and the abolition of compulsory military service; three, the universal security and total preservation of the human species, and of all of the species, through centralized planning and coordination of worldwide natural disaster control measures, with emergency response to sudden and widespread outbreaks of famine and disease; four, an increase in general prosperity by means of a substantial and permanent reduction in the cost of national government, so that the savings so realized can be reallocated to enhance the performance of the remaining functions of government or else retained by the taxpayers of each national or territorial member of the world democratic federal government for additional private consumption and investment; five, an increase in global economic efficiency to its optimal level of performance through the establishing of a universal currency, central bank, and unified system of economic oversight and regulation; and six, concerted action for emerging issues of universal interest, such as environmental protection, with universal protection of vital or endangered species of life, and the exploration and study of the planetary core, polar regions, oceans, atmosphere, and outer space. Let us now turn to a complete examination of the elements of, and the processes for establishing, binding universal law.

# IV.
# Universal Law

World sovereignty, or the inauguration of a world democratic federal government, is the prerequisite, or the necessary and sufficient condition, for the prescription, interpretation, and enforcement of universal law. To see that this is so, we need only to provide answers to three relevant questions. First, "Can there be universal law without a world democratic federal government?" "No, because universal law can not be enforced without some form of a universal government but such a body of law, subsequent to its initial prescription, could neither be appropriately interpreted nor effectively enforced under a universal government other than a democratic federation (since universal law would be invalid either where it could not be ratified by the people who would be subject to it, as under a world government that is not a democracy, or it could neither be uniformly and appropriately interpreted nor impartially and effectively enforced, as under a world democratic government that is not a federation)." Second, "Can there be a world democratic federal government without universal law?" "No, because in the absence of universal law, such a government would neither be valid nor effective." Third, "Can there be universal law outside of (that is, beyond the jurisdiction of) the world democratic federal government?" "No, for the same reason that there can be no universal law without a world democratic federal government, as we have already explained in our answer to the first question." In other words, universal law is meaningless without a universal government; it is invalid within or beyond the jurisdiction of a universal government that is not democratic and equally invalid beyond the jurisdiction of one that is; and it is only suboptimal within the jurisdiction of a universal democratic government that is not also a federation. By the same token, a universal government is meaningless without universal law.

We have said that "utilitarianism, through democracy, can unify the world under one social contract, one government, and one code of universal law to establish permanent peace, thereby insuring the personal security of everyone everywhere." We have also said that "under democracy, society accords sovereignty to its entire membership by means of the social contract . . . an agreement between the members of society that defines and limits the rights and obligations of each person and of society." We have recognized that "the social contract is expressed by means of a constitution . . . a written instrument incorporating the fundamental principles and laws of a nation or other sovereign territory." We have further recognized that "the complete social contract embraces the entire law of the land . . . the aggregate of the federal constitution and the constitutions of each of the constituent governments within the federation . . . also . . . the aggregate of all laws, statutes, and ordinances from all levels of government." Universal law, then, is the social contract and the social contract is the aggregate of all law that is beneficial for human well-being by mutual consent. Each person must agree to the social contract inasmuch as the social contract is an agreement between all persons, that is, a permanent and irrevocable contract between each person and society. If it were not, it could not be binding upon all persons, which is to say, that it could not be relied upon by each person and by society. Accordingly, the introductory clause, or lead portion, of the social contract, the federal constitution, must establish this agreement using language that can, will, and must bind anyone with everyone. This is the most critical element of the social contract and we will discuss it in detail under the designation "social contract ratification." However, much of the law of the land, certainly the greater portion of it, has already been written, has long been upheld in local, provincial, and national jurisdictions, and is openly recorded in the present legislations of all of the various nations and their subpolitical units. This is the main body, or trailer portion, of the social contract, and all that is required of present legislations beneath the federal level of a universal democratic government is that they serve a valid and actual purpose in maintaining or improving the security and well-being of society and that each law and its purpose be communicated in a rational manner so that it can be easily comprehended, not only by those affected in the jurisdiction in which it should apply, but by anyone anywhere. This is the most comprehensive element of the social contract and we will discuss it under the designa-

tion "existent legislation assimilation." Let us turn first to our consideration of social contract ratification.

The social contract can be introduced in the form and language of the
constitution of the world democratic federal government. Like the language of the United States Constitution (which begins, allow us to recall,
"We the people of the United States, in order to form a more perfect union, establish justice, insure domestic tranquillity, provide for the common defence, promote the general welfare, and secure the blessings of
liberty to ourselves and our posterity, do ordain and establish this constitution for the United States of America"), the language of the World
Constitution can be crafted in such a manner as to imply that all of the
people of the world are engaged in creating a social contract by which
they mutually consent to the formation of a universal government to perform all of the necessary and beneficial activities in behalf of all people
that otherwise could not, and would not, be accomplished, neither by
persons working independently nor by those working cooperatively in
particular and limited public or private associations. If the language of
the World Constitution should designate that the responsibilities of government must be to provide for the fundamental security and general
well-being of all of the people, without restriction or exception, and that
the rights of the people, as should be articulated in detail within the body
of the text, are complete, impartial, and immutable, then the instrument
can, and will, qualify as a valid social contract for the entire human species. The authorization for the contract, including the details with respect
to how it should be created, maintained, and interpreted, must come from
the people, either directly—which should always be preferable, except if
it should no longer be generally feasible owing to the immense difficulty,
if not the impossibility, of organizing billions of diverse people to cooperate in accomplishing a common objective—or indirectly, through
elected and appointed representatives.

After the universal social contract has first been authorized and then
written, it must be ratified. Through ratification, the people accept the
complete and final draft. With ratification, the World Constitution, the
universal social contract, becomes valid. Again, the ratification of the
contract, like the authorization for the contract, must come from the people, either directly or indirectly. Since total direct ratification of the universal social contract by the greater portion of over six billion people
(that portion of the world population that can be identified with a universal electorate comprised of all persons of mature and sound mind) is not
very likely to be practicable today, even given the recent extraordinary
advances in the computer and telecommunications technologies that gave

birth, around 1970, to the present Information Age, let us pause to consider how we can effectively refute the argument of those who would
hold that an indirect ratification of the universal social contract can not
be binding upon any of those who, if provided an opportunity to express
a choice, would unequivocally reject the contract.

If a majority of the electorate of a nation has authorized and ratified
the formation of the universal social contract, albeit through the services
of their designated representatives, the objections of those persons who
disapprove of, and consequently seek to disaffirm, the original formation
(or subsequent inheritance or adoption) of the universal social contract
can be overcome through the operation of the legal principle of quasi
contract. If the nation has agreed to enter into a world democratic federal
union and if its citizens have agreed to be bound by a universal social
contract so that the same universal social contract becomes the law of the
land of that nation with the indisputable consequences that the civil
rights of all of the citizens become stronger while the personal security
and well-being of each of the members of society improve, then it must
be construed that no citizen, having received, accepted, and enjoyed the
benefits of the universal social contract, can refuse to be bound by it.
This constructive ratification of the universal social contract will apply
not only to those who did not vote in its favor, whether with respect to its
authorization or its ratification, when it was originally introduced but
also to all of the future citizens of the world democratic federal government who will be born into a world that is subject to the universal social
contract without afterwards ever casting a vote in its favor. Accordingly,
although the universal social contract is, in essence, a contract between
each person and every other person in the world, it will not be necessary
for each person to draw up such a contract, or to sign and date a uniform
copy of such a contract, because of the constructive ratification of the
universal social contract under the legal principle of quasi contract. It
will only be necessary for a majority of the electorates of the nations participating in the original world democratic federation to authorize and to
ratify the initial formation of the universal social contract.

With respect to the assimilation and incorporation into the universal
law of the existent legislations of the democratic nations which will form
the universal democratic federation, whether at its inception or at some
later time, all that is necessary is that such legislations serve as the clear
rational expression of the comprehensive contract between the members
of society for establishing and maintaining those measures which provide
for the general security of person and property and all such other generally agreed upon measures of cooperative action which serve to promote

the general well-being of all of the people. With the adoption of such legislations, the universal social contract will become complete, establishing rational principles of conduct at the most fundamental levels of human existence and interaction through the prescription and proscription of the well-known and long-established mores and taboos of local and regional societies.

Most of this body of law has always been, and still remains, socially useful and beneficial, otherwise it would not have survived the incontrovertible test of long usage, and much of it is expressed in language that is simple, comprehensible, and unequivocal. Nonetheless, the entire legislation of each democratic nation which joins the world democratic federal government must be reevaluated at the time, or within a brief period subsequent to the time, of federation. The legislation must be reexamined to separate and to revise or to eliminate any portions of the law which may be irrational, detrimental, and oppressive (which is to say, the primitive, archaic, and obsolete remnant from an oligarchical past). The remaining legislation must then be redefined, where necessary, so that their purposes and benefits shall be clearly stated.

The legislations of most nations, even those of many modern democracies, were introduced at times that predate the emergence of democracy. Since almost all of the societies and civilizations of antiquity were oligarchies comprised of political and religious elites that imposed sovereignty over the subjugated majorities within their territories, the laws of the early states were generally promulgated through brute force with an immediate and certain threat of severe punishment for those who should dare not to abide by them. The purposes and benefits of these laws were known only to those who created them: the ruling elites or the kings and probably the chief priests and their closest advisors. In most instances, the laws did not express their underlying rationales: where the rationales were not self-evident, they were simply unknown to the majority of the people. The laws expressed only the consequences for disobedience. In many instances, however, the security and well-being of the members of the aristocracy and priesthood depended upon the political and economic stability of the entire society. Accordingly, the laws were often useful and beneficial for a large number of the people and sometimes, even the majority.

Modern democracies will be required to redefine and to restate the laws which they have inherited from previous governments where such laws do not express their underlying rationales (unless, of course, such laws, at some point, have already been revised and recast). The laws must be expressed as if they were written not by an elite group but by every person in society. This process of legal transformation is absolutely essential so that the laws of society can be understood, accepted, and observed by all persons. The process may be thought of as a kind of a moral translation of the law from its original dogmatic proclamation to its ultimate rational expression. Furthermore, this process must reexamine every piece of existent legislation, even those laws which appear to express an underlying rationale or otherwise to be "self-evident." To the greatest extent which may be possible, the language employed for the rational expression of universal law should not only be clear, comprehensible, and unequivocal, but always consistent in its logical application and generally uniform in its literary style. Accordingly, even such traditional laws which appear to express an underlying rationale or otherwise to be "self-evident" will likely need to be redefined and restated.

Once the entire body of law within each democracy has been provided a uniform rational expression upon each democracy's entrance into the universal democratic federal union (or within a reasonable period of time thereafter, certainly no longer than about one hundred years, even where the accomplishment of the objective may prove to be most difficult), it will remain to bring into agreement the diverse legal systems that may have been incorporated into the universal government. Both political philosophy and political science must support the development of the discipline of jurisprudence, including the recruitment of a sufficient number of multinational legal theorists and practitioners to optimize its ultimate and essential contribution to the ongoing maintenance of world peace. The discipline of jurisprudence must assume an unshared burden to develop over the coming one hundred to five hundred years an effective and permanent universal legal system to supersede the four major, but largely incompatible, legal systems that are currently prevalent throughout the world (civil law, common law, Islamic law, and Marxist-Leninist law). In the end, the new universal legal system must provide an apparatus for the effective and efficient administration of universal law by means of uniform and ubiquitous legal procedures that will be accessible to everyone everywhere.

Finally, it will become necessary to create a universal judicial body to function as the ultimate authority in the interrelated processes of administering and interpreting the law of the unified human society that must soon come to be governed by its own members through the world democratic federal government. If the name that will emerge to identify the universal government should become known as, say, the United Democracies of Earth (the name for the new government that I recommended in my previous book *Toward World Sovereignty*), then the name that should emerge to identify the highest judicial body of this government will very likely be the Supreme Court of the United Democracies of Earth. This universal supreme court should be created by an article of the constitution of the world democratic federal government. The creation of the universal supreme court will be an essential and integral part of the universal social contract. The functions of the court must be to decide cases in which a member nation is a party or which affect an ambassador to, or from, an autonomous state. The court must also serve as the court of final appeal for cases arising from either the lower regional and appellate federal courts of the world democratic federal government or the supreme courts of the member nations. The universal supreme court, then, will be in both an appropriate and an exclusive position to arbitrate controversies of the greatest complexity or of universal concern with immediate and universal effect.

In keeping with the principle of the separation of powers, the number of the judges on the court and the lengths of their terms of office should be predetermined by the world federal legislature while the appointment of judges as vacancies arise must remain the prerogative of the current chief executive officer, subject to confirmation by the legislature. When a decision of the court fails to pass the test of time, meaning that it creates a detriment of greater magnitude than that of the benefit that it was intended to create, or of the detriment that it was intended to alleviate or to eliminate, the legislature must retain the right to reverse the decision through new legislation or, where relevant, constitutional amendment. In addition, the impeachment of judges who engage in criminal activity, or who otherwise neglect to perform the duties of their office in a manner that is useful and beneficial for society, must at all times remain an option which may be exercised at the discretion of the legislature.

As in similar matters with respect to the creation of the world democratic federal government, the cumulative experience of the government of the United States of America can serve as a reliable and worthy model in the matter of creating and maintaining the universal supreme court. We would earnestly recommend that this example of the American government be conscientiously followed, at least in its greater part if not in the whole.

Having touched upon its essential particulars, including a simple and feasible plan of procedure, we may bring to a close our discussion concerning the drafting of the universal social contract and the simultaneous creation of binding universal law. At the same time, we bring to a close our consideration of the first two of the four principles that comprise the philosophy of symbiosism, the principle of noninjury and the principle of utility. This, then, brings to a close our consideration of the first half of the philosophy of symbiosism, the half that is concerned with objectivity, with consensus, with universal compliance, with providing and maintaining private, public, and environmental security, and with promoting the happiness of human beings as a whole. Our consideration of the second half of the philosophy of symbiosism will open with a discussion of the third principle of symbiosism, the principle of beneficial reciprocity. We will follow this with a discussion of the philosophy that is predicated upon the principle of beneficial reciprocity, the philosophy of reciprocitarianism, the philosophy which I propose as the optimal means to achieve personal happiness. We will follow this in turn with a specific discussion of that element of reciprocitarianism that is applicable to all human beings, the element of benevolence, the element which unites the philosophy of reciprocitarianism with the universal and allows it to transcend becoming nothing more than a philosophy of egoism, favoritism, or particularism. This discussion, a reciprocitarian discussion of universal benevolence, will serve as a counterpart to the utilitarian discussion of universal law which we have just concluded. The discussion will then be followed by a discussion of the fourth principle of symbiosism, the principle of magnanimity. The principle of magnanimity retains much of the ethical ideals of the ancient Greeks and Chinese, of Aristotle and Confucius, of the ethics of nobles and heroes. In this spirit, it is retained as an ethical ideal for all of the people of the world, both in the present and in the future. As such, it will benefit society with the contributions of exceptional individuals and reward exceptional individuals with the honors of society. The discussion of the principle of magnanimity will bring to a close our consideration of the second half of the philosophy of symbiosism, the half that is concerned with subjectivity, with personal freedom, with diversity of taste and opinion, with the matters of the heart, and with promoting the happiness of human beings as autonomous individuals. The two halves of the philosophy of symbiosism, objectivism and subjectivism, are complementary ethical forces, the first in essence bringing benefit to society, the second, to each person. The truly moral person is he or she who stands at the intersection of objectivity and subjectivity in the ethics of symbiosism. We will return to this central idea at the conclusion of the book.

# V.
# The Third Principle of Ethics—
# Beneficial Reciprocity

It can not be denied that the principles of noninjury, beneficial reciprocity, and magnanimity proceed from, and are specific and limited applications of, the principle of utility. I have maintained that utilitarianism is essentially a highly objective social ethics, ideally formulated to function as the measure of optimal ethical value and performance for the activities of groups of all kinds, including families, social organizations, occupational and professional associations, corporations, and governments. Now, perhaps we can agree that it is always best, on the one hand, not to inflict injury upon any innocent sentient being and, on the other, to do whatever is useful and helpful for all (or, at least, the greatest possible number of) innocent sentient beings. However, even John Stuart Mill, who conceived of utilitarianism essentially as a kind of personal ethics, acknowledged that justice requires only a general obligation to practice noninjury. In chapter five, "On the Connection Between Justice and Utility," of *Utilitarianism*, he writes:

> Justice implies something which is not only right to do, and wrong not to do, but which some individual person can claim from us as his moral right. No one has a moral right to our generosity or beneficence, because we are not morally bound to practice those virtues towards any given individual.

We can infer, then, that the acts of any given person to maximize pleasure and to minimize pain according to the principle of utility may, and most likely will, be planned and performed by that person in such a manner as to give the highest priority to maximizing personal happiness and minimizing personal unhappiness. An increase in the well-being, and/or a decrease in the deterioration of the condition, of other sentient beings (including, of course, an increase in the happiness, and/or a decrease in the unhappiness, of other people) will certainly and necessarily attend the acts of almost any particular person, but the number of such persons or other sentient beings in part will depend upon the intentions of that person, upon his or her abilities, and upon chance. For this reason, any application of the principle of utility, considered as a typical application of "private utility" rather than "public utility," will be better considered as an application of the principle of beneficial reciprocity. At the same time, any application of the principle of utility, considered as an atypical and noble application of "private utility" rather than "public utility," will be better considered as an application of the principle of magnanimity. From this point forward, each of these principles will be considered independently of (although, in a very real sense, each principle has been essentially derived from) the principle of utility.

Succinctly stated, the principle of beneficial reciprocity holds that only by initiating beneficial behavior towards others can one induce others to behave towards oneself in kind, thereby creating for oneself the greatest possible pleasure and happiness with the least possible pain and misery. In an attempt to understand the rational underpinnings of this principle, let us examine an analysis of interpersonal behavior within the context of an image of elemental and primeval society. Interpersonal relationships in such a society may be classified as including those between equals and those between unequals, that is, between the strong and the weak. Let us continue by first considering the latter.

Our analysis of interpersonal behavior in the most typical Old Stone Age society, among one of the earliest tribes, clans, or families of hominids, between the members of any given migratory group subsisting as hunters and gatherers when not obliged by the vicissitudes of weather to take temporary shelter in caves, will refer to certain modes of habitual behavior for which we will do best from the outset of our discussion to establish clear and precise definitions. An outline of the basic concepts of such primitive behavior follows.

When one person initiates behavior that affects another person, we will call this kind of behavior "initiatory" behavior. Such behavior either will be of a kind that can be described as pleasant, helpful, useful, encouraging, and/or protective, that is, of the kind that we will call "beneficial," or of a kind that can be described as unpleasant, harmful, abusive, oppressive, and/or punitive, which is to say, of the kind that we will call "detrimental." (Let us note, of course, that in either case, we are talking about a benefit for, or a detriment to, the person who is affected by the initiatory behavior.) When a person responds to initiatory behavior, whether such behavior is beneficial or detrimental, his or her response either may be reciprocal behavior, that is, behavior returned in kind, which we will call "reciprocity," or nonreciprocal behavior, which is to say, behavior returned not in kind, which we will call "nonreciprocity." Whether the response is reciprocal or not, it will also be beneficial or detrimental (that is, beneficial for, or detrimental to, the person who initiated interpersonal behavior in the first place and who in turn becomes affected by responsive behavior). Therefore, while there are only two kinds of initiatory behavior, there are four possible kinds of responsive behavior whenever a response is induced. If an initiatory behavior is detrimental and the response is in kind, we will call the response "detrimental reciprocity" (also known as "retaliation"); if an initiatory behavior is detrimental but the response is not in kind, we will call it "detrimental nonreciprocity" (also known as "appeasement"). If an initiatory behavior is beneficial, we will call a response in kind "beneficial reciprocity" but a response not in kind "beneficial nonreciprocity." In summary, then, we have six modes of interactive interpersonal behavior: beneficial initiatory behavior, detrimental initiatory behavior, beneficial reciprocity, detrimental reciprocity, beneficial nonreciprocity, and detrimental nonreciprocity. Let us proceed to consider the various motives which give rise to interpersonal behavior of all kinds, including the six aforementioned and predefined interactive modes.

During the Old Stone Age, which denotes the earliest phase in the cultural development of the members of the various genera and species of Hominidae and which commenced at an indeterminate moment over the past one to two million years to comprise the prehistorical component of the Pleistocene epoch within the Quaternary period of geological time, the social behavior of the hominids was most likely, in most respects, very little different from that of the great apes: the chimpanzees, the gorillas, and the orangutans, those closest relatives of man among the animals. The social organization of Pongidae (and, at the time of the Old Stone Age, of Hominidae as well) generally consists—at the simplest level, in the family—of a single powerful and dominant adult male; perhaps one or two other adult males; two, three, or four adult females; and a small number of offspring of both sexes. Rivalry between adolescent and adult males to attract the pubertal females and then to establish a permanent social arrangement is so intense that unsuccessful males often either are killed or driven away to live by themselves on their own. Interpersonal relationships between male rivals is such, then, that the stronger males generally engage in detrimental initiatory behavior towards the weaker males, often resulting in the death or flight of the weaker males. If the weaker males are able and willing to offer a response, that response is generally in the form of detrimental reciprocity (or retaliation), which also often results in the death or flight of the weaker males. The counter-response of the stronger males again is one of detrimental reciprocity and we can see that a cycle of violent and abusive interpersonal behavior is thereby set in motion that persists until the stronger males have established their supremacy.

Another possible response by the weak to the detrimental initiatory behavior of the strong sometimes arises in the form of detrimental nonreciprocity (or appeasement), which often results in pacifying the strong so that they will tolerate the presence of the weak without engaging in further aggression toward them. We may call this turn of events "extortion and appeasement," wherein the strong succeed in establishing their supremacy over the weak by intimidating the weak and then extracting from them a sign that they have accepted domination by the strong. The weak are permitted to remain in the group, to make contributions to, and to draw benefits from, the group, unless and until they should mount a challenge to the supremacy of the strong at some future time. Thus, at least among the adult males, the strong effectively establish their supremacy by eliminating rivals in the constant struggle for power under the law of nature.

Now, among the other members of the group, the adult females and the offspring, the same struggle for power also prevails, although it is considerably milder and much less ferocious than that which is common between adolescent and adult male rivals. The adult females dominate the offspring, both male and female, and among the offspring, the larger and older dominate the smaller and younger, regardless of gender. Accordingly, some individuals emerge as strong and domineering, others as weak and submissive.

As for the weak, they can only hope to try to prevent the strong from inflicting injury upon them. They can not induce the strong to behave beneficially toward them since the beneficial behavior of the weak toward the strong, whether initiatory or responsive, is generally interpreted as appeasement.

If the weak within a group are so at the mercy of the strong, why do they stay? Because of either of two reasons. First, any given group usually includes more than two individuals, that is, more individuals than one who is strong and one who is weak. Therefore, one who is weak can dominate others who are even weaker in the same manner that the one who is weak is dominated by those who are strong, unless the one who is weak is among the very weakest members of the group. Second, an individual's relative strength changes over time, such that that individual is most weak when very young or very old, most strong when in the prime of life. Therefore, it is optimal and beneficial, even necessary, for the weak to stay with their groups when they are very young until they become self-sufficient, by which time, of course, they will also have become strong enough as adolescents or adults to dominate an entire new generation of offspring or, for the adult males, to challenge anew the supremacy of the alpha male.

To recapitulate our analysis of interpersonal relationships between unequals in a group of people living at the time of the Old Stone Age, we have seen that the strong generally engage in detrimental initiatory behavior to establish or to maintain their supremacy over the weak. If they were to let down their guard and to engage in beneficial initiatory behavior, they would quickly become vulnerable to attack from the sudden and treacherous beneficial nonreciprocity of opportunistic rivals. Although the relationships between the alpha male and the adult females of his harem are never as volatile as those between the adult males, still the relationships exhibit a degree of detrimental initiatory behavior sufficient to establish and to maintain limits upon the freedom of the adult females. Accordingly, beneficial initiatory behavior is seldom evident in the relationships between unequals, with one significant exception. Beneficial initiatory behavior generally characterizes the relationships between a mother and her offspring, at least from birth to the time of weaning and often for an extended period beyond weaning until the youngsters have acquired a certain degree of self-sufficiency. Undoubtedly, the explanation for this sole instance of beneficial initiatory behavior among unequals is the mother's identification of her offspring with herself: it is a form of self-serving behavior, just like eating and sleeping. We should further note that the behavior of the offspring in response to the behavior of the mother is the only evident instance of beneficial reciprocity in the interpersonal relationships between unequals. As we have already observed, the most common responses and counterresponses to the interpersonal behavior of unequals include detrimental reciprocity (retaliation) and detrimental nonreciprocity (appeasement).

The interpersonal relationships between equals is another matter. In an Old Stone Age familial or tribal group, there are never as many equals as unequals. Those that will be present must include individuals of equivalent size and strength and such individuals, of course, are most likely to be found within the same categories of age and gender. Just as with the interpersonal relationships between unequals, equals may engage in detrimental initiatory behavior toward other equals, perhaps inducing a retaliatory response that causes, in turn, a retaliatory counterresponse. In such a scenario, we can recognize that a cycle of violent and abusive interpersonal behavior will have been set in motion that will likely persist ad infinitum, equals being equals. This cycle can be avoided or interrupted only with either the death or flight of one of the equals or a response or a counterresponse of detrimental nonreciprocity (appeasement).

On the other hand, equals may engage in beneficial initiatory behavior (which is almost never seen in the relationships between unequals, except for those between a mother and her offspring). This possibility arises because of the higher incidence of injury which befalls equals (vis-à-vis that which befalls the strong) when they engage in detrimental behavior toward each other. In this situation, the recipient of the benefit may, or may not, decide to respond. If the recipient does respond, the response must take either of two forms: it may take the form of beneficial nonreciprocity (which may be regarded as, depending upon the magnitude of the response and/or the timing of its incidence within a cycle of interpersonal behavior, either an expression of rejection or an act of treachery) or it may take the form of beneficial reciprocity. If the recipient has decided upon the former response, returning evil for good, the donor may still offer a counterresponse that is not in kind, persisting to engage in beneficial behavior by returning good for evil, although this is the least likely course to be chosen. The donor is much more likely to walk away from the recipient or even to offer a counterresponse that is in kind, thereby increasing the likelihood of precipitating a cycle of violence and abuse. If the recipient has decided upon the latter response, the donor then will find himself or herself in the same position as that in which the recipient had previously been placed. If he or she then responds in kind, a cycle of mutually beneficial behavior can be set in motion that should persist ad infinitum.

We may conclude our analysis of interpersonal behavior in the social world of early man with the following observation. Unlike the plight of the weak within the power relationships between unequals, equals are never at the mercy of each other. If they choose detrimental behavior, whether as initiatory or responsive behavior, they incur a risk of defeat, including their own death or flight, that is equal to their opportunity for victory, including the death or flight of their opponent. Therefore, for each equal, an unfavorable outcome is just as likely as a favorable one.

Sooner or later, it becomes painfully obvious that detrimental interpersonal behavior exacts too high a price to pay for coping with the presence of one's peers. Alternatively, if they choose beneficial behavior, whether as initiatory or responsive behavior, they can induce the other equal to behave beneficially in response or counterresponse. If the other does not, another may be found who does. Such behavior will incorporate the different strengths (but not the weaknesses) of the equals. Since, for each equal, such behavior is more worthwhile than not, it is more likely to be chosen than not. So it is that we can trace the origin of the principle of beneficial reciprocity to two sources: the love of a son or a daughter for his or her mother, which is natural, and the propensity for cooperation among peers, which is rational.

Even through the beginnings of civilization and recorded history, human societies have perpetuated the interpersonal relationships of inequalities and of equalities such as appear to be quite similar to those prototypes which we currently can observe and describe among troops of the great apes and which we also can somewhat confidently ascribe to the earliest families of human beings. Among the relationships of inequalities, aristocracies and priesthoods (comprising, by and large, relatively small groups of the most powerful, intelligent, and able of men aligned, both through marriage and various other familial relationships, with the most beautiful, engaging, and wellborn of women) superseded the alpha male while, taken together, the various lower classes within the typical oligarchical societies of early civilization, comprising the vast majority of the people, can certainly be recognized as analogous to that subgroup comprising the remaining members of the primordial human family. Not until modern history, particularly from the time of the Age of Enlightenment, with the ascendence of the law of reason over the law of nature and the accompanying triumph of democracy and capitalism, first in North America and Western Europe, and then throughout most of the world, have interpersonal relationships between unequals decreased in a substantial measure, where they have not generally disappeared altogether, so that interpersonal relationships now include only, or virtually only, those between equals wherever societies have rejected oligarchy. During the continuing course of national democratization with the inevitable inception of world federalization and the concurrent progressive emancipation of individual human beings from the onerous and artificial constraints of unjust and antiquated cultural norms, four of the six traditional modes of interactive interpersonal behavior most likely will quickly become fully obsolete except for very specific applications in maintaining the fundamental security and vitality of society without compromising the personal freedoms of its members. We can reasonably expect these applications wherever residual inequalities remain. We can readily identify three such inequalities: those between teachers and their students, between physicians (or other health care providers) and their patients, and between law enforcement officials and criminals. The first of these affects everyone when he or she is young; the second, many people of all ages whenever they should become seriously ill; the third, only those few persons who choose to violate the laws which safeguard the lives and properties of all people. In every instance, those with power employ a system of rewards and punishments, in other words, the promise of benefits and the threat of detriments, to induce desirable behavior and to control undesirable behavior among those without power. This kind of activity has always been, and still appears to be, necessary to insure a secure, healthy, and educated society. Nonetheless, it must remain our heartfelt and incessant hope that continuing improvements in interactive interpersonal behavior, including continuing progress in social reform, will one day eliminate altogether the need for punishment, thereby effectively precluding appeasement and substantially reducing all of the modes of detrimental behavior. The only modes of interactive interpersonal behavior, then, that are generally appropriate for human beings living and working together throughout the age of the law of reason are beneficial initiatory behavior and beneficial reciprocity. Furthermore, as we shall soon begin to understand with a greater degree of clarity, only the private adoption and practice of an ethics of reciprocitarianism, predicated as it must be upon the principle of beneficial reciprocity, can enable the ordinary individual to attain the greatest possible magnitude of personal happiness during his or her lifetime. As we have now completed our presentation of its underlying principle, let us proceed to discuss the functional details of this moral philosophy.

# VI.
# Reciprocitarianism

Antecedents of the ethics of reciprocitarianism can be found among various elements of classical Chinese philosophy, first in Confucianism at about 500 B.C., then even more powerfully in Moism approximately one hundred years later.

Confucius lived at a time in China that was little different from that later time in Rome, during the days of Ovid and Augustus, when the people no longer could take seriously their traditional gods and goddesses or otherwise derive meaning from the religion passed on to them by their forefathers. His philosophy marks a definitive transition in Chinese civilization, from animism and polytheism to humanism and monism.

The seven cardinal concepts of Confucianism include *T'ien* (Heaven, or moral destiny); *Tao* (the Way, or natural process); *Te* (Integrity, or human conformity to the Way); *Li* (Ritual, or etiquette); *Yi* (Duty, or an adequate observance of etiquette); *Shu* (Reciprocity, or a sharing of beneficial experience); and *Jen* (Humanity, that is, humaneness, or benevolence). In introducing the concept of *shu*, Confucius anticipated the principle of beneficial reciprocity. He has provided the earliest known articulation of the "Golden Rule":

> Adept Kung asked: "Is there any one word that could guide a person throughout life?"
> The Master replied: "How about *Shu*: never impose on others what you would not choose for yourself?" (*The Analects* XV.24)

The Confucian concept of *jen* is quintessential to Confucian ethics. Within the concept of humanity is incorporated a number of moral principles, including humility, compassion, courtesy, mutual understanding, and beneficial reciprocity. The distinctive Chinese character for *jen* is a compound formed by combining two other characters, one representing "human being," the other, the number "two." It suggests all that constitutes, or can contribute to, beneficial and desirable human interaction, including all of the relevant knowledge and decisions which support such an interaction. In discussing the concept of *jen*, Confucius suggests the ethics of reciprocitarianism:

> Adept Kung said: "How would you describe a person who sows all the people with blessings and assists everyone in the land? Could such a person be called Humane?"
>
> "What does this have to do with Humanity?" replied the Master. "If you must have a name, call this person a sage. For even the enlightened Emperors Yao and Shun would seem lacking by comparison. As for Humanity: if you want to make a stand, help others make a stand, and if you want to reach your goal, help others reach their goal. Consider yourself and treat others accordingly: this is the method of Humanity." (*The Analects* VI.29)

At the time of his death in 479 B.C., Confucius was 72 and, by this time, he had taught and influenced a total of approximately 3,000 pupils and disciples (according to tradition), who resided not only in his home principality of Lu (now the province of Shantung) in northeastern China but in several of the neighboring principalities through which he traveled during the final decade of his life. Some of his pupils were men of means, from aristocratic families, and almost all were drawn from the most talented, ambitious, and/or highly recommended among Chinese youths, candidates accepted and trained to serve as ministers and administrators for the rulers of the principalities within the empire. In this sense, Confucius was a teacher in ancient China not unlike Plato or Aristotle in ancient Attica or Macedonia, a tutor in behalf of, if not always directly in the service of, the aristocracy.

Mo Tzu was born in China just nine years after the death of Confucius, in 470 B.C. One could surely assert that the two philosophers are in fundamental agreement with respect to the essentials of their respective ethics; it is only with respect to certain of the details, primarily the critical determination of which one, or ones, among the various concepts should bear the greatest emphasis, that they are not always in agreement.

Mo Tzu adopted the concept of *jen*, even expanding it into an ethics of universal love. At the same time, he affirmed the principle of utility, by which he rejected the Confucian concepts of *li* and *yi* as useless and wasteful. Earlier, we acknowledged the philosophy of Mo Tzu as the fountainhead of utilitarianism. We may now, with considerable justification by virtue of his ethics of universal love, also look to Mo Tzu, in addition to Confucius, as one of the very few thinkers at the dawn of the age of the law of reason to grasp the full significance of reciprocitarianism. In Section 16, "Universal Love" (Part 3), of *The Book of Mo Tzu*, he writes:

> Among the books of the former kings, in the "Greater Odes" of the *Book of Odes*, it says:
> There are no words that are not answered,
> No kindness that is not requited.
> Throw me a peach,
> I'll requite you a plum.
> The meaning is that one who loves will be loved by others, and one who hates will be hated by others.

Similar antecedents of reciprocitarianism can be identified with the concept of universal love as proclaimed independently in different parts of the world at the beginning of the Christian era by two of the current five major world religions, Buddhism and Christianity.

Siddhartha Gautama, the founder of Buddhism, lived and taught in India at about the same time as Confucius in China. (He was born twelve years before Confucius and lived eight years longer, to the age of eighty.) The first significant accomplishment of Buddhism, which was set in motion during Siddhartha's lifetime but not fully realized until the emergence of Mahayana Buddhism some five centuries after his death, was to introduce the concept of egalitarianism in religion. Siddhartha taught that the practice of dharma, that is, engaging in the process of attaining liberation from the recurrent sufferings experienced during the endless cycle of birth, death, and rebirth, is open to any person who might be willing to attempt it (thereby liberating the process from the control of a priestly caste). The second significant accomplishment of Buddhism, which also was not realized until the emergence of Mahayana Buddhism, was to introduce the concept of universal love in religion. The Mahayana school taught that the practice of dharma was no longer exclusively a personal effort but that it had gradually become a social effort wherein the bodhisattvas, those who have attained enlightenment, defer the ultimate attainment of liberation, or nirvana, for an indefinite period during which they assist others to attain enlightenment. The persons who are closest to attaining liberation, then, begin to exhibit a tendency to become selfless, to love those who are not as close in reaching the goal, and to assist others along their personal paths.

The universal love advanced in Buddhism is quite obviously not very much unlike the love of parents. A mother and a father love their children, who, in turn, grow up to become mothers and fathers who love their own children as well as their parents, who have now aged and will eventually, if they have not already, become ill and disabled. In this kind of love, we can recognize a love of unequals, wherein those possessing a sufficiency of power of a certain kind love those who are deficient in power of the same kind. (Adults in the prime of life love both the very young, who have not yet attained the full mental and physical powers of adulthood, and the very old, who have lost much of their previous vigor. There is operating in this situation a kind of double reciprocity: a direct reciprocity, in which the son or daughter repays the parent for the care received during childhood when the parent has grown too old to remain fully self-sufficient; and an indirect reciprocity, in which the son or daughter repays the parent by giving love to children of his or her own. This double reciprocity unites three successive generations in families, binding grandparents with grandchildren.) With respect to the love of unequals in Buddhism, we can further recognize without any difficulty that the magnitude of one's capacity to love other people is directly related to the extent of one's progress in attaining enlightenment.

On the other hand, the universal love advanced in Christianity is both a love of equals as well as a love of unequals. Accordingly, it is a kind of universal love sharing more in common with the teachings of ancient Chinese philosophy than with those of Buddhism. The Christian concept of universal love is undeniably the most influential of the antecedents of reciprocitarianism. We must even admit that it is the very fountainhead of reciprocitarianism in the Western world. No other antecedent has had such a profound effect upon the modern mind. The Golden Rule, in the form that typically comes to mind, was expressed by Jesus as follows:

> As ye would that men should do to you, do ye also to them likewise. (St. Luke 6:31, King James version)

The concept of reciprocity was further developed in a subsequent passage:

> Give, and it shall be given unto you . . . For with the same measure
> that ye mete withal it shall be measured to you again. (St. Luke 6:38)

Finally, on the occasion of the Last Supper, Jesus explicitly admonished his disciples always to practice beneficial reciprocity. Through this admonition, he also introduced to the world his concept of universal love:

> A new commandment I give unto you, that ye love one another: as
> I have loved you, that ye also love one another. By this shall all men
> know that ye are my disciples, if ye have love one to another. (St. John
> 13:34, 35)

We can see that the ethics of reciprocitarianism is as old as Jesus, Mo Tzu, Confucius, and the Buddha. Yet each of the philosophies or religions established by these extraordinary men presents an incomplete and inadequate formulation of the ethics. Each inadequacy presents a specific moral problem. We will attempt to explain these problems as we develop our discussion of reciprocitarianism.

The moral problem for religion is that the ethics of a religion are predicated upon the metaphysics of the religion. Regardless of whether or not the ethics of religion has a basis in reason, it always remains dependent upon the metaphysics of religion, which has no basis in reason. Since reason can not tell us whether or not God exists, or whether or not there is life after death, we are left with insufficient grounds to know or even to presume that the benefits we provide for others during our lifetimes will ever somehow be rewarded after our deaths. This problem is essentially the same whether we are considering Buddhism or Christianity. Of course, if the ethics of a religion, considered independently of the religion, can be seen to have little or no basis in reason, then it must be rejected. It is a different matter, however, when it can be seen to have a substantial basis in reason. Then it can be accepted, or at least considered, in its own right. This criterion has enabled me to establish my position with respect to the interpersonal and social aspects of the ethics of Christianity. I have long valued the ethical teachings of Jesus, both as they have been directly expressed in the New Testament Gospels of the Bible and as they are generally interpreted today in the Christian religion. Throughout all of my previous work in moral philosophy, I have assiduously attempted to rediscover the rational foundation of the ethics of Christian love so that others could easily recognize that such an ethics forever stands firmly upon its own support. I have also attempted to demonstrate that the ethics indisputably is not unique to (in other words, that it is not the exclusive property of) Christianity, inasmuch as the essential qualities of Christian love, either in full or for the most part, are also present in Confucianism, Moism, and Mahayana Buddhism. It has been of the utmost importance for me to succeed in demonstrating this distinction because the concept of Christian love, in combination with earlier concepts of love (in contemporary Christianity, the progressive series of such concepts is often designated by the Greek terms *eros*, *philia*, and *agape*, with *agape* defining the highest, the noblest, the most advanced concept of love, the concept of Christian love, the brotherly love of a universal kinship), can be effectively practiced by, and can provide unprecedented benefits for, all of the people in the world throughout their lifetimes: non-Christians as well as Christians, including Jews, Muslims, Hindus, Buddhists, adherents of less well-known religions, unbelievers, and atheists. Almost without exception, the various qualities of Christian love (humility, good will, charity, compassion, forgiveness, loyalty, and pacifism) in combination with earlier and more rudimentary concepts of love (friendship and romantic, or erotic, love) provide the very substance of the ethics of reciprocitarianism.

In my earlier books, I have generally referred to the ethics of reciprocitarianism as "the value of love," meaning by that term a personal value system wherein a person chooses to love others as the optimal means to induce others to assist him or her in satisfying the needs and desires of life and in averting its dangers and hurts. During the time that has passed since I first used the word "love" in this particular sense, I have become increasingly concerned about the high level of ambiguity stemming from the ordinary usage of the word "love" in the English language today. At once, "love" can be understood to mean a physiological urge, an emotion, and an idea, and, as an idea, we are already familiar with the diversity of interpretations which have evolved. In my opinion, every other word in English is totally inadequate for providing a precise definition of this ethics. Accordingly, I have finally come to the conclusion that it is now necessary to replace the term "the value of love" with a new one that can be considerably more accurate in communicating the intended meaning, even if such a term can not be acquired except at the cost of coining a new word. Since the personal ethics of which we speak is essentially predicated upon the principle of beneficial reciprocity, we may propose henceforth to refer to it exclusively as the ethics of "reciprocitarianism." At the same time, we should do well to seek a more precise definition of this ethics so that both the new term and its intended meaning can endure in complete agreement.

We could very simply state that reciprocitarianism is that form of ethics predicated upon the principle of beneficial reciprocity, whereby one initiates beneficial behavior towards others so as to induce others to reciprocate in kind. Just as simply, we could also state that reciprocitarianism is that form of ethics predicated upon the Golden Rule, whereby one behaves towards others in a way that he or she would like others to behave toward him or her.

I would like to offer the following as an equally broad and (hopefully) a somewhat superior definition, admittedly under a risk of sacrificing simplicity for a higher level of clarity. Reciprocitarianism is that form of ethics wherein people endeavor to behave towards one another in a manner that is intended to induce beneficial reciprocity whereby to facilitate the satisfaction of the fundamental needs of life and to establish or to maintain adequate safeguards against as many as may be possible of the myriad hurts of life.

Having stated our formulation of the most appropriate working definition of reciprocitarianism (a definition that is similar to, if not synonymous with, any definition of Christian love, albeit expressed in psychological rather than in supernatural terms), let us proceed to consider the various phases and categories of reciprocitarianism. These are four in number but the first which we will examine is the same as the one which we first experience during the course of life. It is, of course, the reciprocity of unequals.

Previously, while considering the social behavior of our primitive ancestors, we ascertained that, in general, the only instances of beneficial initiatory behavior or beneficial reciprocity between unequals occurred between a mother and her children. Furthermore, we concluded that the reason behind this anomaly was that the mother identified her babies with herself (at least from birth or perhaps even from the time that she was first conscious of her pregnancy until the time that she came to recognize that her children were no longer dependent upon her) so that she took care of her babies in the same manner that she took care of herself. The beneficial initiatory behavior of the mother is a natural phenomenon that is widespread among, and characteristic of, mammals. We have even come to refer to this phenomenon as "the maternal instinct," and to the extent that we can determine with the utmost certainty that it truly is a natural instinct, even where it is evident among human beings, we can also conclude that this kind of behavior transcends reason. A similar inference can be drawn with respect to the cause of the most rudimentary forms of beneficial reciprocity of the offspring (such as cuddling and caressing) since the offspring just as certainly identified their mother with themselves as the mother identified themselves with herself.

Nevertheless, we can easily see, and must frankly acknowledge, that all of the forms of human beneficial reciprocity beyond the most rudimentary are learned responses. Examples include smiling, kissing, hugging, and, occurring sooner or later in one's social development, speaking certain courteous words and phrases as appropriate, like "please?", "may I?", "thank you!", and "you're welcome!" Now, with respect to the natural phenomenon of human reproduction, the differentiation of unequals between those who are powerful and those who are weak is such that the father and all others who share in taking care of the child can be associated with the mother in comprising the class of the powerful while the child, along with his or her siblings, if there are any, remain to comprise the class of the weak. The beneficial initiatory behavior of those who are involved with the care of the child can best be described as "nurture." On the other hand, since the child is in no position to provide a return in kind to the parents, the response of the child can only be an expression of gratitude, and the parents have generally taught the child to communicate this emotion by demonstrating deference to the parents and, in addition, to all other adults familiar to, or even admitted into the presence of, the child. Thus interpreted in, and from, the course of its origin, the beneficial reciprocity of the child, or children, can best be described as "honor."

This natural cycle of beneficial initiatory behavior and beneficial reciprocity among unequals, the cycle of "nurture" and "honor," originates in earliest childhood and continues throughout the process of maturation, during which the child learns how to think, how to do things on his or her own, and how to get along; during which the child learns to take on more and more responsibility, to demonstrate that he or she is gradually becoming more and more reliable, and to develop intellectual, occupational, and social skills; until, eventually, the child transmutes into a fully grown, independent, and self-actualizing young adult, one who gives even as one takes, and one who is no longer an unequal among unequals. There are, however, certain inequalities among human beings other than the given natural inequality of parent and child. Broadly speaking, such inequalities appear wherever an individual is distinctly deficient in some manner or condition vis-à-vis his or her peers. They can arise at any moment within the span of life. They include inequalities in health, law-abidingness, and education, with associated relationships wherein one party accepts a responsibility for, and assumes a burden of, assisting another party, who is deficient in some respect, to alleviate or to correct the deficiency. One kind of these relationships is that between physicians and patients (extending to that between caretakers and the chronically and terminally ill or the elderly disabled); a second kind, between law enforcement officials and criminals; and a third, between teachers and students. As in the relationships between parents and children, those who are powerful, or self-sufficient and able, provide nurture (which is to say, that they attempt to satisfy others' needs or to remove others' deficiencies) while, in return, they receive honor. The converse holds true for those who are weak, or deficient and dependent: they receive from others the wherewithal to correct their deficiencies while, in return, they honor their benefactors. Now, almost everyone will agree that while it is most generally true that students honor their teachers, it is far less certain that patients always honor their physicians and most doubtful that convicted criminals ever honor those who enforce the law. My position in the face of the common opinion of the degree to which beneficial reciprocity should, or should not, be present as typical responsive behavior in relationships among the various categories of inequalities conforms with the common position of a small number of diverse philosophers, including Confucius, Socrates, and Sartre, who maintain that we all need to think and to act with a higher level of honesty (especially to liberate ourselves from all forms of self-deception), to take full responsibility for our decisions and actions (or for our failure to decide and to act), and to change for the better all things that are changeable. With respect to the promulgation and enforcement of basic criminal law, I wholeheartedly believe that we must introduce sweeping measures to make education in the law a required component of the curriculum of elementary education in all democratic nations and to require continuing education in the law for all convicted criminals in the same nations during the entire period of their incarceration until their rehabilitation into society becomes complete. Inasmuch as the relationships between unequals, other than that between parent and child, affect us all (however indirectly, remotely, or potentially), we must attempt to formulate a rational point of view with respect to the various parties of those relationships. We will return to this issue a little later during the course of our discussions of benevolence and universal benevolence.

The other phases and categories of reciprocitarianism involve the reciprocity of equals. They are present wherever the universal has superseded the particular, wherever cognition has ascended to an adequate level of human self-awareness, and wherever people have accepted their common humanity. These are the relationships of humanity with itself. They include the relationships of one with oneself, of one with all others, and of one with specific representatives (some given, some chosen) of all others. These relationships are progressive, such that one must honor the humanity that is within and the humanity that is without before one can move on to become a good friend to anyone in particular. We will examine them momentarily, one at a time, beginning with self-esteem. Beforehand, however, let us briefly digress to reconsider those antecedents of reciprocitarianism which arose in ancient China.

Unlike the ethics of religion, classical Chinese moral philosophy is in no sense associated with, or dependent upon, an irrational metaphysical foundation. The moral problem for classical Chinese philosophy is that the latter of the two major schools advocating universal love arose, developed, and culminated as an absolute, rather than as a complementary, moral philosophy. Confucianism advocates the love of man for man but emphasizes preferential love (the love of subject for ruler, of spouse for spouse, of child for parent, of sibling for sibling, and of friend for friend) while Moism advocates the love of man for man without any emphasis upon preferential love. As we shall come to understand, the Chinese would have done better to embrace both philosophies (if only the two philosophies had been presented in such a manner that such a decision could have been possible) rather than to accept Confucianism and to reject Moism since, in substance, the two philosophies are not at all contradictory but complementary.

The problem of a universal love with no allowance for some form of preferential love, which we must recognize as the central issue of Moism in contradistinction to Confucianism, is bipartite. The first half of the problem is the problem of moral dilution: the effectiveness of the sum of anyone's gifts of goods and services to other people, if evenly distributed, will diminish in inverse proportion to the number of donees. Viewed as such, universal love is both inefficient and ineffective, although it remains the most just expression of love. In this sense, the problem of universal love is not unlike the problem of democracy, where pure democracy is always optimal but generally impractical, requiring a concession to representative democracy. The second half of the problem is the problem of inadequate reciprocal reinforcement between the love donor and any given donee. Recurrent beneficial reciprocity between the same two people provides happiness of a kind and of an intensity that is generally unattainable by any other means. It follows, then, that for any given person, under the assumption that one never permits imagination to betray reason, the practice of universal love without any accommodation for some form of preferential love is, must be, and always will be, unappealing, undesirable, and unworkable.

On the other hand, the problem of a universal love which emphasizes preferential love, which we must recognize as the central issue of Confucianism (at least as it came to be interpreted and advanced by Mencius and Hsün Tzu), is the problem of injustice, or exclusion, in love. This problem is also bipartite.

The first half of the problem involves exclusion within one's group. It appears in any number of forms, including nepotism, cronyism, and various other kinds of opportunistic favoritism. The second half of the problem involves indifference to, or exclusion of, people outside of one's group. It also appears in any number of forms, including unconcern, aloofness, and even xenophobia. Now, by definition, no love that is essentially exclusive can also be universal. It follows, then, that for everyone everywhere, any practice of universal love that emphasizes preferential love is at once unjust and incomplete.

We should now be able to see that where each of the two classical Chinese moral philosophies was ultimately unable to succeed on its own, neither one could have ever failed if it had been so modified as to have been presented and promoted in combination with the other. The relationship of one with all others must be such that it is able to accommodate the relevant needs of human beings in their existence as autonomous individuals and as equal members of the universal human family. Accordingly, it must require universal benevolence to an extent that is optimal for preventing injustice while it must also permit the unqualified exercise of individual free will for the personal pursuit of happiness through friendship.

We have recognized that the four phases and categories of reciprocitarianism include one that is the reciprocity of unequals (involving the activity of those who are powerful to nurture those who are weak and deficient, with the reciprocal activity of those who are weak and deficient to honor those who have provided nurture) and three that comprise the reciprocity of equals, that is, the integral parts of the relationship of humanity with itself, to wit, the relationships of one with oneself, or self-esteem; of one with all others, or benevolence; and of one with certain others, or friendship. We have also recognized that both self-esteem and benevolence must be present before friendship can occur. Self-esteem and benevolence can occur once one becomes physically, emotionally, and intellectually mature, once one has become independent and self-sufficient, once one is no longer an unequal among unequals. It must be one of the fundamental responsibilities of those who provide nurture to promote and to develop self-esteem in those for whom they provide nurture so that those who are weak and deficient can, and will, eventually

become strong and competent. If the nurturers should succeed in fulfilling this responsibility, their charges will one day be prepared to think, to
decide, to act, to relate, and to attain and to retain happiness, through efforts and accomplishments of their own.

Children do not see value in themselves unless, and until, those who
care for them first see their current and/or potential value and then make
a deliberate effort to inform them about the perceived evidence that sup-
ports a present certainty, and/or a future probability, that certain of their
actions possess, or eventually will come to possess, such value. Once
children have grown up to become independent and self-sufficient, they
finally will have become capable of seeing value in themselves without
requiring, and relying upon, the assistance of others. Once they have arrived at this level of consciousness, we say that they have attained self-
esteem.

What is it that we mean when we say that we see value in ourselves
or that we help others to see value in themselves? Just what is this
value? Surely, it is nothing more than whatever we do that is useful for
others in some respect, whether we are talking about something useful
that we do for others, or something useful that we create and make and
then provide to others. In either event, others commonly will so compen-
sate us for our services and goods that we will easily acquire the wherewithal to meet our own personal needs. We know, then, that we have
value because others tell us that we have value, and even from the earliest time that we became aware that we do not yet have value, we quickly
learn from others that we always have a decided potential to acquire and
to increase value.

We could attempt to do everything for ourselves, to reject the contributions of others, to become exclusively self-sufficient. Nevertheless, to
the extent that others are helpful and not harmful, cooperative and not
obstructive, worthy and not worthless, our lives will be safer, healthier,
richer, happier, and longer if we should offer our contributions to others
and accept their contributions in return.

This is what we mean when we talk about the relationships of humanity with itself: the relationships of one with oneself and of one with
all others, of seeing humanity within oneself as well as oneself within
humanity, of being at once the indiscrete whole and a discrete part of the
same whole. To love people, one must respect people. One must have a
high regard for oneself as well as for all other people. One must almost
always have complete confidence in oneself and a generally high level of
confidence in all others. In reciprocitarianism, a person behaves toward
others as he or she desires others to behave in return. Before this can

happen, one must think of others as highly as one thinks of oneself, and one must also think of oneself as highly as one thinks of others. Accordingly, reciprocitarianism commences with a complete self-esteem that must embrace infinite benevolence, and an infinite benevolence that must include complete self-esteem. The consciousness of humanity that acknowledges at once the value of the humanity within and the humanity without, of the one and the all, of the individual and the species, is the very essence of reciprocitarianism. Upon this foundation, reciprocitarianism functions effectively as care. There are four distinct aspects of this mode: concern, regard, justice, and beneficence. Let us consider them successively.

We should begin by recalling that we always repudiate maleficence, whether we may make our judgment as victim, witness, or simply a matter of principle, inasmuch as we have long since concluded that no good can ever issue from a voluntary and unlawful injury. Accordingly, we also always repudiate detrimental reciprocity, even when we are a victim, or we possess some affinity with a victim, of maleficence. In repudiating injury, we resist provocation where we must while we avoid it where we can so that we will neither retaliate nor suffer unnecessary interruption of our equanimity. All instances of our repudiation of maleficence are essentially rational and volitional, whether we are a victim of, or a witness to, an injury or otherwise we simply stand on principle.

Likewise, concern, the first aspect of care, is essentially rational and volitional, whether it should be directed inwardly as a component of self-esteem (where it may be called self-interest) or outwardly as a component of benevolence (where it may be called goodwill). In either event, we have made a decision to do good, both in behalf of ourselves and in behalf of all others. From the moment of our decision, we carry forward an intention, or a disposition, to do good, both for ourselves and for all others. We wish ourselves the very best and we wish the very best for all others, whether we are able, with or without assistance, to realize our wishes in full or only in part. The three remaining aspects of care are not only rational and volitional but active.

Regard, the second aspect of care, involves communication. We form a favorable opinion of ourselves and of all others, and then we communicate that opinion to ourselves and to all others. When we are talking only of ourselves, this kind of regard may be called self-respect; when of all others, courtesy. The degree to which people practice courtesy varies considerably from one culture to another and, within certain cultures, it has also varied considerably from one age to another. Whether the practice of courtesy should comprise a highly elaborate code of decorum or simply a minimal set of signs and conventions (including a license for all signs that may be original, spontaneous, and unique, on condition that, notwithstanding, their intended meanings are unequivocal) is a consideration which we will explore and develop in the next chapter. For the time being, let us tentatively recommend that each person practice such courtesy as may be indigenous within his or her particular culture and then extend the same courtesy to the remainder of humanity.

We must never underemphasize the importance of courtesy in interpersonal communication. Courtesy is the foundation of love. Courtesy is the first sign, and sometimes the only sign, of benevolence. Without courtesy, the door is closed to justice, beneficence, friendship, and loyalty. Without courtesy, the door is open to resentment, revulsion, injustice, and malevolence.

One further matter requires our attention. While the practice of courtesy must be equal and universal, there is a reason, one which does not actually offend against justice, to practice a courtesy of a stronger degree toward a specific subgroup of society. We have said that, in the reciprocity of unequals, the proper response of those who have received nurture is to honor their nurturers. Since all of us as children require nurture from those who care for us; since most, if not all, of us as children and/or as adults occasionally require the assistance and guidance of teachers and health care practitioners; and since even a few, if not so very many, of us as adults require the intervention of law enforcement officials if we have failed to abide by the law, our proper response as members of society, both as equals and unequals, in all of these forms of the reciprocity of unequals, is to honor the nurturers of society. Accordingly, it should be useful, beneficial, and never at all unjust if everyone were to extend a higher degree of courtesy, that is, to pay honor, to those who teach, enforce the law, or provide care in behalf of those who are ill or the elderly disabled. Such universal honor is unexceptionally appropriate because everyone benefits from the fruits of education, not just those who have been educated; everyone benefits when the law is upheld, not just those who have been prosecuted, disciplined, and rehabilitated; and everyone benefits when the standards of health care in society are high, not just the elderly disabled or those who have been healed of sickness or injury.

Justice, the third aspect of care, requires honesty and fairness in one's relationships. When one is dealing only with oneself, one is required to be fair to oneself, not to deceive oneself (or, as Sartre has put it, to recover oneself from living in *mauvaise foi*. Since "we are what we are not and we are not what we are," we will always move closer to that which we are capable of becoming, provided that we affirm our potentiality: it is only when we deny our potentiality that we are being unfair to ourselves or, as it were, living in *mauvaise foi.*) When one is also dealing with others, one is required to be fair to others. Such fair play has both universal and particular applications. Specifically, it requires honesty and impartiality in one's actual dealings with others. Generally, it requires sustaining a relentless intolerance for injustice, demonstrated by continuous and active participation in various cooperative efforts to reduce and to eliminate injustice.

Beneficence, the fourth aspect of care, involves doing good for oneself and for all others. In doing good for ourselves, we desire to assume full responsibility for ourselves so that we should never become a burden upon others. Our objective is to achieve self-sufficiency and it is by this term that we may best think of this kind of self-centered beneficence. In doing good for others, we engage in activities which promote human well-being. In this situation, we are no longer equals among equals but have become unequals among unequals. However, most of us will not be members of the specific class of nurturers (the health care practitioners, teachers, and law enforcement officials) but self-sufficient persons who desire and act to assist in some meaningful and effective manner the indigent, the downtrodden, and the hopeless. We may best think of this kind of altruistic beneficence as charity. It requires our commitment of personal assets: our gifts of service, goods, and financial resources. In general, because of the problem of moral dilution, this aspect of care is only effective when it is accomplished in concert with similar efforts by many others, when the number of recipients is rather small, and when the magnitude of the needs of the recipients is somewhat modest. Otherwise, charitable activities will only be effective when engaged in by governments and other social organizations which command an adequate magnitude and variety of resources. Certain individuals may also qualify to engage in effective charitable activities but such individuals will be exceptional human beings by virtue of their superior talents, great wealth, and/or extensive influence. In this situation, we must take leave of reciprocitarianism altogether and enter into a new moral domain, the ethics of magnanimity. We will have more to say of this in due course.

Friendship is the fourth and final category (the third of the three phases and categories that comprise the reciprocity of equals) and the fourth and highest phase of reciprocitarianism. Friendship largely resolves the bipartite problem of universal love: the problem of moral dilution inseparably coupled with the directly related problem of inadequate reciprocal reinforcement. Through friendship, our care and concern can deeply affect the lives of those immediately closest to us: our family, friends, neighbors, coworkers, and acquaintances. The strength of our close relationships is determined by their degree of intimacy, which, of course, is determined by the strength of our affection and commitment. In our earliest years, we experience a great happiness and a close intimacy with our parents and siblings. As we mature, we seek out our potential spouses—those favored and chosen particulars among a valued and given universal—with whom we can establish our own homes and families to recreate for ourselves and then to attempt to sustain for the remainder of our lives that great happiness and close intimacy which we had experienced as children. In addition to our parents and siblings, our spouses and children, and our children's spouses and children, we form meaningful, albeit less intimate, relationships with friends, neighbors, coworkers, and acquaintances with whom we feel a special attraction or share a common interest. Some of our relationships are determined by chance, or nature, such as the families into which we have been born and the families into which our siblings, our children, and our grandchildren marry. Other relationships are created through the exercise of our own freedom of choice, such as our decisions to marry, to have children, and to form and to maintain various other friendships. All of these relationships arise from a combination or a reciprocity of determinism and free will where they do not arise exclusively, whether in whole or in part, from one or the other of the two sources of causation. For example, let us contemplate that we may freely choose to have a child, and if we are healthy and fertile and if we conceive within the appropriate stage of life and phase of the reproductive cycle, we will likely give birth to a child, but whether we give birth to a son or a daughter will largely, if not fully, depend upon chance, or nature. Nonetheless, in all of our relationships, we can freely choose to exert a direct or, at the very least, an indirect effect upon another person, or a number of persons, by being a good friend.

It remains for us to describe the various qualities of friendship. They are seven in number, accumulative, and, like the practicable sequence of formal study in the technical training of a fine artist, best presented in the order in which they normally appear in the development of friendship.

The first quality of friendship is understanding, meaning both to come to an understanding of the person who we care about and to communicate our findings to that person so as to assist him or her in coming to a better understanding of himself or herself. This quality arises in the combination of the great commandment of Judeo-Christian tradition ("You must love your neighbor as yourself") with the Socratic injunction ("Know yourself") and, reduced to a maxim, the sense of this quality can be readily conveyed by the words "You must know your neighbor as yourself." In the event that some among my readers may remain skeptical as to the fundamental importance of understanding in friendship, please permit me to offer an elucidation in the form of a series of rhetorical questions. First, "Can one love another without first possessing self-esteem?" Second, "Can one attain self-esteem before one comes to know oneself?" Third, "Can one actually love one's neighbor before one comes to know one's neighbor?" Fourth, "Does not the most rudimentary expression of friendship consist in assisting one another to come to know one another?" Fifth, "Do all persons involved not stand to benefit from the intrinsic reciprocity of this process?"

The second and third qualities of friendship, encouragement and advice, are very closely related. The one provides emotional support; the other, intellectual guidance. At any given time, and depending upon the nature of the recipient, his or her situation, and the friendship itself, the one may be received more willingly and appreciatively than the other. In either event, one must proceed with care in these expressions of concern, always bearing in mind that courtesy and respect precede friendship, establishing the very foundation for all acts of friendship. First, a good friend must quickly discern whether his or her providing encouragement and/or advice will actually be welcome and helpful. Then, he or she can, and may, act accordingly.

The fourth quality of friendship is the integral quality, or unity, of apology and pardon: apology, as the simultaneous admission of blameworthiness and expression of regret directed to an injured friend by one who, in some manner, whether intentionally or unintentionally, and whether directly or indirectly, has injured his or her friend; pardon, as the expression of the injured one's willingness to give up any resentment of, or claim to redress for, the injury caused by his or her friend when that friend has offered an apology; pardon, as the only appropriate and effective response to, and reciprocity for, an apology so as to restore both the integrity and the mood of the friendship; apology and pardon en suite, as the inescapable means to reconnect the isolated semicircles of a sadly and badly broken circle of friendship.

Like the second and third qualities, the fifth and sixth qualities of friendship, generosity and assistance, are very closely related. With generosity, one provides gifts for one's friend on occasion as an expression of kindness and affection. Such gifts may be expected (as is customary when commemorating special occasions, such as birthdays, graduations, weddings, wedding anniversaries, religious festivals, and the like) or unexpected. The frequency and the costliness of the gifts generally vary in direct proportion to the thoughtfulness and the wealth of the donor. With assistance, one provides gifts for one's friend when one's friend is in need. As with generosity, the extent of such assistance generally varies in direct proportion to the thoughtfulness and the wealth of the donor. We can clearly see that the friendship qualities of generosity and assistance depend upon the same pleasure–pain principle that underlies the ethics of utilitarianism. In generosity, we endeavor to create pleasure for our friends with the hope that they will reciprocate like pleasure for ourselves in the future. In assistance, we help our friends through difficult times with the hope that they will do the same for us if we should fall upon hardship in the future.

The seventh and the supreme quality of friendship is loyalty. With loyalty, one's understanding of, and support for, one's friend is obvious, uninterrupted, and lifelong so that, subject only to death itself, one's friend will always enjoy an ultimate recourse and will never be hurt by an abrupt denial of access to reliable mental and material support.

Friendship, then, arises in mutual understanding, progresses through a course of giving and receiving in return, or receiving and giving in return, and consummates in loyalty. Beyond these general observations of the qualities of friendship, we have nothing further to say, inasmuch as friendship is essentially subjective, not objective; a habit, not a methodology; and an art, not a science.

We would do well at this point, however, to reconsider a phase and category of reciprocitarianism, one somewhat less subjective than friendship, that we discussed immediately prior to our brief description of the qualities of friendship. We are referring, of course, to that portion of the relationship of humanity with itself that involves the general relationship of any given human being with any of all other human beings, and the term that we have been using to denote this specific kind of relationship is benevolence. Benevolence simply means a resolve to care about other human beings. A benevolent person, then, is a caring person. We have said that the four aspects of care in benevolence include goodwill, courtesy, fair play, and charity. Now, from the point of the origin of the human species through the present time, except all of that tiny minority of people today who we refer to as the magnanimous, this kind of human self-consciousness has seldom extended, nor seldom extends, beyond the boundaries of the largest group to which any given human being has felt, or feels, himself or herself to owe allegiance. The continuing prevalence of such groups reveals the persistence of particularism, inasmuch as these groups typically include nations, religions, races, castes, and political and economic classes. Early on in the course of this book, however, we advanced the argument that man has crossed over from a condition of living exclusively in the age of the law of nature to one of living concurrently in the age of the law of nature and the age of the law of reason, the presence of the latter being clearly and jointly indicated by the ascendance and globalization of scientific technology and the ascendance of the universal over the particular in human self-consciousness. Accordingly, that critical initial phase of reciprocitarianism that is concerned with caring about other people must extend beyond the limits imposed by one's aloofness or unconcern, beyond the range of one's acquaintances and other direct encounters with the public, and beyond the boundaries erected through one's inclusion within a particular group, to embrace the entirety of the human species. Benevolence, then, must be universal, and it must be universal not only as a precept, but as a norm; not only in theory, but in practice; not only by right, but in fact. Unlike universal law, universal benevolence is slightly possible in the absence of a world democratic federal government since, as we have seen, it is already a fundamental attribute of those few extraordinary persons who we refer to as the magnanimous. Nevertheless, the universal practice of universal benevolence will remain very difficult, and even the decision to embrace benevolence will remain highly problematic, for the great majority of the people of the world wherever the particular has failed to yield to the universal. Accordingly, we must discuss universal benevolence within the context of a unified world, of world sovereignty, of the world democratic federal government and the society within its jurisdiction. We are now prepared to continue with such a discussion.

# VII.
## Universal Benevolence

We have said that universal law depends upon the inauguration of a world democratic federal government. The same holds true for universal benevolence, but for a different reason. Universal law is highly objective and can neither be effectively embraced nor enforced except within a universal jurisdiction. Universal benevolence is highly subjective, yet it will be virtually, if not absolutely, ineffective until the emergence of a world democratic federal government. This is so because of the continuing problem of cultural identity preference, otherwise known as discrimination. Throughout the past, human beings have generally tended to favor the members of the group or groups to which they belong. At once, whether consciously or unconsciously, one may favor the members of one's race, nation, and/or religion. We can readily see the practical constraints upon the practice of universal benevolence within the parameters of race and nation. Only religion liberates the practice of universal benevolence, particularly Mahayana Buddhism and Christianity, but we have already recognized the inadequacy of religion in providing a rational foundation for morality. But even should we fail to take this into account, we must acknowledge that the obvious general contradiction between national loyalty and religious loyalty largely nullifies, restricts, or, at least, interrupts the effective practice of universal benevolence. It follows, then, that no one will fully embrace universal benevolence until one becomes a voluntary member of a unified world community, which is to say, until one becomes a citizen of, or enjoys the benefits of citizenship in, a world federal union of national and territorial democracies.

We have also said that infinite benevolence (which is synonymous with universal benevolence) functions effectively as care (which is syn-

onymous with love—in the broadest sense of the word as it is commonly
used in the English language). The four distinct aspects of care that are
relevant to infinite benevolence are goodwill, courtesy, fair play, and
charity. Now, benevolence arises in intention, reveals itself through
communication, and ultimately expresses itself through action. We can
see, then, that care is a process and we shall come to see that communication is at the heart of this process.

Initially, my intention may not be immediately communicated to
others: I decide to care about other people but I neither directly nor explicitly inform others of my decision; instead, as I encounter other persons, I treat them with courtesy, which is to say that I am considerate of
their needs, desires, and feelings. Incorporated in the very concept of
courtesy, then, is the related concept of friendliness since the bipartite
purpose of the communication is not only to attempt to prevent maleficence (by avoiding any effrontery or disregard that might incite detrimental reciprocity and thereby initiate a recurring cycle of ill will, effrontery, and injury) but to reveal goodwill (that is, to initiate an
unfolding of benevolence) and thereby to attempt to prevent any misunderstanding. Accordingly, goodwill by itself, present only as undisclosed
intention, is about as useless as an unopened bottle of very good table
wine: it becomes beneficial only once the cork has been pulled.

Courtesy and friendliness reveal goodwill. If a person should encounter one hundred people in a day or a week, he or she may be friendly
toward only ten or fifteen of them while little or no more than merely
courteous toward the other eighty-five or ninety. Friendliness arises in
courtesy and advances an interpersonal relationship to a new and higher
level, to a degree of interaction that is richer in emotional satisfaction,
more intimate, and more reciprocal. But courtesy is valuable in ethics not
only because it constructs the most direct and reliable path to friendship
but because it precipitates the initial and most fundamental catalysis of
interpersonal harmony. Since the practice of courtesy is of such moment
for human beings in our communications and dealings with one another,
the teaching of courtesy must become a major priority in the moral training of the young along with education in the ethics of noninjury and the
fundamental psychosocial and biospheric concepts of equity. In the past,
the teaching of courtesy, of good manners, of decorous conduct, was
primarily accomplished in the family but it was common only among the
upper and middle classes, that is, in polite society. The majority of the
people, who occupied the lower classes, learned whatever they could of
courtesy directly through their associations (and then only in proportion
to the extent of those associations) with people of good breeding.  The

practice of courtesy, then, tended to filter down from the top of society to the bottom. The responsibility for the moral training of the young in a fully democratic society must be different. It must pass from the province of the family into that of public education. We must urge sweeping reforms in general education in all of the societies that will come to comprise the nascent world federation of democratic nations. Explicit federal standards in moral education must be established and maintained to provide effective universal training in the ethics of noninjury and the concepts and practices of courtesy and fair play. Such training must be uniform regardless of cultural differences. When the children and the young people of the world have been raised to practice noninjury, courtesy, and fair play, human society will gradually become transformed in such a way as to insure and to increase personal security, prosperity, and happiness everywhere.

We must also urge similar and related sweeping reforms in criminal prosecution. The aforementioned reforms in general education should certainly create their effect upon the overall incidence of crime after the passing of a generation or two, but we should not expect to reduce crime solely through the introduction of universal public moral education of the young. (Human beings will never lose their possession of free will; consequently, we can expect only to reduce, not to eliminate, harmful and dangerous social deviation.) Rather, we must extend universal public moral education beyond the periods of childhood and adolescence for those persons who have been convicted of crime. This form of continuing moral education must take place during the period of the sentence or, specifically, the period of incarceration, when the convict is being rehabilitated for eventual reentry into society. In advancing this approach to the public prosecution of crime, with its liberal interpretation of the purpose of punishment within the process, we gratefully acknowledge our indebtedness for the pioneering efforts and influences of the great social reformers who emerged during the Age of Enlightenment, most notably Rousseau, Beccaria, and Bentham. We would firmly recommend that all prisons within the various jurisdictions of the coming world democratic federal government be provided with sufficient classrooms and teachers so that convicted criminals will have every opportunity to come to accept responsibility for their personal behavior, to learn from their past mistakes, and to go forth to enjoy a new opportunity to seek, and perhaps to find, happiness in life without causing injury to themselves, to others, or to the physical environment. Furthermore, we would strongly urge that this opportunity always be made equally available to habitual criminals as well as first offenders; consequently, hope, which fuels the relentless pursuit of happiness among all human beings, need never succumb to present reality.

It may be noted that in pressing for sweeping reforms in general education and criminal prosecution in the democratic society and government of a unified world, we may appear to have temporarily digressed from a discussion of that phase and category among the reciprocity of equals in reciprocitarianism that identifies the constructive relationship between the one and the all (that is, the texture of initiatory and reciprocal behaviors that gives substance to infinite and universal benevolence) to reconsider some aspect of the relationship between nurturers and their charges in the reciprocity of unequals. Since such an observation certainly is neither invalid nor ignorable, we would like to demonstrate that the digression is in fact quite necessary and bears a strong relevance to the discussion which is at hand. We have said that the appropriate reciprocal response of the nurtured is to convey honor to the nurturers. In the infinite benevolence that ought to be practiced by all of the members of a unified world community, we would lastly recommend that all members of society, not just those who receive nurture, convey honor to the nurturers of society inasmuch as everyone benefits—individually, at one time or another; collectively, at all times—from the skills, efforts, and dependability of the nurturers. All of society, then, would do well to convey honor to the educators; to the physicians and the various other providers of health care; and to the law enforcement officials and the various other rehabilitators of convicted criminals. The nurturing professions must become the most honorable occupations in society since they are instrumental in transforming a democratic society into an egalitarian society. Only through the assistance of the nurturing professionals will parents be able to fulfill their responsibilities to their children. Only through the efforts of the nurturing professionals will the unequals among unequals in society ultimately become transformed into equals among equals. The rich emotional rewards received by the nurturers from the voluntary and collective implementation of this social reform should supplement the substantial financial rewards (which should already have been, presently be, or soon begin to be) flowing to them. This reform will do much and go far to encourage learning, to sustain optimal health, and to increase security.

Open and unbiased friendliness with the wholehearted and effective practice of courtesy within a unified world community will greatly ameliorate the psychosocial problems of isolation, whether those who may be isolated should reside in various remote localities of the world democratic federation or of the discrete autonomous states. In this respect, let us recall that we have easily established the obviously preponderant ethical value of courtesy and we have clearly demonstrated that it is absolutely necessary to induce interpersonal harmony. We should also note that it is always incontrovertibly helpful, if not always absolutely necessary, to sustain interpersonal harmony.

It remains for us to consider the appropriate expression of courtesy in a democratic society and whether, or under what conditions and in what circumstances, it must be formal or may be informal. Our discussion will proceed from an analysis of the origin of the practice of courtesy.

Let us begin by positing a somewhat stark axiom. As a general social principle, originating in prehuman history and sustaining itself through tradition and instinct despite the ascendence of reason in human affairs, unequals attract while equals repel. In the primeval family, the alpha male either killed, drove off, or cowed his rivals, leaving only his unequals. The alpha male then tolerated the continuing presence of unequals as assistants in the relentless struggle to procure the necessities of life. A symbiotic relationship developed among the members of the group, such that the weak depended upon the leadership of the powerful while the powerful depended upon the coalescent collective strengths of the weak. Nevertheless, the weak demonstrated their inequality with the alpha male by deferring to him. This primeval deference is the origin of courtesy. Such deference signified that an actual or potential rival of the alpha male was effectively cowed. Without such a signal, the weak either would have been killed or driven away from the group. Did the powerful initially teach deference to manipulate the weak or did the weak initially practice deference to mollify the powerful? The answer, most likely, is that the weak initiated the practice of deference as a mechanism for defense and survival. By means of deference, the fundamental relationship of inequality was quickly established and permanently sustained in human society.

This fundamental relationship of inequality, then, with its characteristic practice of deference, has persisted throughout the entire course of human existence. It is seen in every human family, where the relationship between parents and their children is almost always one of unequals among unequals. It is also seen in every oligarchical society, where the relationship between rulers and subjects is generally one of unequals among unequals.

Although the practice of deference undoubtedly originated with the weak, I believe that, over time, its form was steadily modified and gradually improved during the process of interaction between the powerful and the weak. Ultimately, courtly behavior, or the practice of courtesy, had become customary among the members of the aristocracy while the observance of good manners was becoming increasingly prevalent among the members of the upper and middle classes.

We can foresee that the practice of good manners by the children in most families is very likely to continue and we have already talked about the unquestionable need for everyone to honor the nurturers of society, but what are we to say about the need for the universal practice of courtesy in a democratic world society, a society of equals among equals? Simply this: that whereas the practice of courtesy is generally necessary for those who are dependent and generally unnecessary for those who are independent, the equals among equals in a democratic society are neither fully dependent nor fully independent but interdependent. Accordingly, the practice of courtesy must remain necessary for them, but not to the extent of the traditional practice of courtesy by unequals among unequals. The practice of courtesy must be merely sufficient to prevent aversion. The expression of courtesy must be adequate to communicate the presence of goodwill as well as the absence of either ill will or indifference. With the effective practice of courtesy by everyone, neither effrontery nor intentional neglect will remain possible. With the sincere practice of courtesy, dishonesty will become impossible. Since the function of the practice of courtesy is no longer to appease those who may have the capacity to injury but to prevent the aversion of those who may have the capacity to help, the practice of courtesy need no longer be ceremonious, formal, nor even conventional, provided that it always be effective and sincere. We would recommend retaining diplomatic protocol to prevent even the slightest tactlessness and consequent misunderstanding between governments but it may be hoped that it will one day become possible to deformalize the practice of courtesy among governments.

Once courtesy and friendliness reveal goodwill, it becomes possible to realize benevolence through action. In this context, there are two kinds of action: one, to eschew and to prevent dishonesty and interference in the legitimate affairs of others, which is to say, to promote justice; the other, to promote beneficence, that is, to do good for others. One activity is as fundamental to universal benevolence as goodwill and courtesy: with the other, universal benevolence can extend to its optimum. One activity is indirect and remedial; the other, direct and supportive. One participates in removing obstacles; the other, in bearing burdens. We call the one activity "fair play"; the other, "charity." We need now to provide a few brief comments on these moral qualities of the bona fide life, the functional activities of universal benevolence, the active aspects of care.

The injuries which occur when one person deliberately harms another fall into either of two categories. In one, the injuries are obvious and direct, as when a person commits murder, assault, rape, arson, extortion, robbery, or theft. These comprise the injuries of crime. In the other, the injuries are nonobvious, as when, in a business transaction, a person exchanges too little for too much; insidious, as when a person offers heroin to an addict or a child; or indirect, as when a person interferes with another's lawful endeavors to earn a living or calumniates another in an attempt to ruin his or her successes, opportunities, and interpersonal relationships. These comprise the injuries of injustice and inasmuch as they are just as damaging as the obvious and direct injuries, they must be treated, if they have not already been so treated, as the injuries of crime. The injuries of injustice, whether nonobvious, insidious, or indirect, do not truly fall under the ethics of reciprocitarianism: along with obvious and direct injuries, they comprise prohibitions that quite obviously fall under criminal or civil law in addition to the ethics of noninjury and, in consequence, are enforced by the courts of law or equity.

However, if any among the injuries of injustice do not fall under extant criminal or civil law, one has a moral obligation not only not to commit such injuries but to eliminate and to prevent the conditions which give rise to them, either through personal or cooperative action where such injuries appear to be highly anomalous and therefore very unlikely to recur, or by lobbying to enact corrective legislation where they do not. In the latter situation, the unjust injury may effect individuals who, except for being victims, have nothing else in common with each other, or it may effect all or most members of a particular class of people. In either event, the fundamental human rights, or civil rights, of the victims have been ignored and violated. (These rights arise from the very premise of the principle of noninjury. The argument is quite simple and may be expressed as follows: in adhering to the principle of inflicting no intentional injury upon others, I am sharing in a common adherence to the very same principle by all other people; therefore, I can reasonably expect not to be intentionally injured by any other person. My fundamental obligation as a human being gives rise to my fundamental human right: to be secure of any intentional injury, whether to my person, property, or freedom, caused by any other human being. At the same time, my fundamental right as a human being gives rise to my fundamental human obligation. The obligation can not exist apart from the right, nor the right apart from the obligation. The principle of noninjury, with its inherent reciprocity of obligation and right, is the sovereign maxim of ethics. It is the foundation of symbiosism.) Where the unjust injury effects the members of a particular class, whether the differentiation is predicated upon race, nationality, ethnicity, religion, occupation, age, gender, sexual orientation, or any other objective criterion, the fundamental civil rights of the members of the class must be both observed under the ethics of noninjury and protected under the laws of society. If the civil rights of the members of such a class are not currently protected by law, one has a moral obligation under the principle of fair play to become active in promoting legislation to establish and to protect these rights, thereby effectively and permanently eliminating one categorical incidence of injustice in society.

In the present world, much remains to be accomplished with respect to promoting fair play between the citizens of one nation and those of other nations. It should become far less difficult to practice fair play once it becomes possible to establish, and to enforce the protection of, universal human rights upon the eventual inauguration of a world democratic federal government.

Who will deny that charity is the ultimate and greatest act of benevolence? Charity entails all of one's efforts to assist without compensation those who are continuously in need or who have suddenly suffered a great misfortune. When people are continuously in need, we will most likely do best to try to help them to help themselves. But what are we to say of those who have suddenly suffered a great misfortune? If any should question what good it can do when a person of limited means endeavors to be charitable toward those who have fallen into distress, we would request that we be allowed to argue each of three possible responses.

First, whereas the individual charitable contributions of persons with modest resources must necessarily be of limited value, the collective contributions of the same persons acting in concert can accrue to a substantial amount. For this reason, spontaneous public outpourings of charity directed to the hapless victims of natural disasters are generally very effective in relieving suffering. While the introduction and implementation of a plan to provide or to guaranty insurance for disaster relief will surely come to be universally recognized as a valid function of the government of a universal democratic federation, we can expect that the constituency of a world society will also come to recognize that optimal disaster relief must proceed from a combination of benefits originating in both the public and private sectors of the global economy.

Second, a certain person by chance may be the only one available to assist the hapless victim of a sudden misfortune at a particular time in a given situation. No one else may be available to serve in the place of this person during such a window of opportunity. The relieving of suffering, and perhaps even the saving of a life, may not otherwise be accomplished without the charity of this person. Is this not the meaning of the Christian parable of the Good Samaritan?

Third, when we are benevolent towards those in distress, we can feel reasonably confident that other persons may be benevolent towards us if we should fall into distress. Is this, along with friendship, not the consummation of reciprocitarianism?

Charity lies at the intersection of reciprocitarianism and the ethics of magnanimity. Any determination of whether charity should fall within the province of the one or the other will require an acquaintance with its magnitude and frequency. It must suffice that most people must restrict their practice of symbiosism to the ethics of noninjury, utilitarianism, and reciprocitarianism since only the most extraordinary of people will ever be able to be magnanimous. It is appropriate now to present the ethics of magnanimity, to reveal how it rewards those who practice it, and how it rewards society.

# VIII.
# The Fourth Principle of Ethics—Magnanimity

To introduce the ethics of magnanimity, allow me to return to the dialectical method which I employed in the introduction to my book. I will attempt to answer the critical questions relevant to magnanimity which may be most likely to arise among those readers who have remained with me to this point.

The first of these questions, "What is magnanimity?" Most simply stated, my answer must be "Magnanimity is the way, or the ethics, of one who is, or of those few who are, magnanimous."

Second, "Then what does it mean to be magnanimous?" "It means to act not as an ordinary person but as a great person."

Third, "How does a great person act differently from an ordinary person?" "An ordinary person looks after oneself and, in varying lesser degrees, those closest to oneself, and although such a person may also wish to help others, he or she will generally lack the ability to give effect to the desire; a great person, on the other hand, not only looks after oneself and those closest to oneself (one's family, close friends, and associates), but such a person is both willing and able to help others: in short, such a person is altruistic."

Finally, "Then what does it mean to be altruistic?" "The person who is altruistic lives not only for himself or herself but for other people (for all other people, or as many other people as possible, or at least some other people other than those closest to oneself); such a person acts not only in one's own interests, or in the interests of those closest to oneself, but in the interests of others: indeed, such a person identifies his or her own interests with the interests of others. Moreover, altruism is generally ineffectual unless it is practiced by those who are magnanimous, since only the magnanimous are able to look after the needs of others while neglecting or even impairing their own interests."

My answers to the hypothetical questions about magnanimity which I can imagine that you would ask if we were engaged in an active dialogue reflect and inform a long-established awareness of a select ethics of magnanimity. Let us examine this tradition of magnanimity as it emerged in ancient history, first in China and a little later in the Greco-Roman world.

In ancient China, both Confucius and Mo Tzu gave voice to the idea that the proper object of moral conduct ought to be to advance the general well-being of all people; both of these philosophers maintained that such a mode of personal conduct should not be all that difficult for all or most people to adopt; yet both of them clearly admitted that most people generally do not like to do those things that they ought to do. (Perhaps this uneasy conjunction of an expression of reason and an evaluation of experience is the earliest recognition of that perennial and puzzling conflict between reason and emotion that has comprised the central intellectual concern of the civilized world over the past two centuries. Perhaps the potentiality for, if not always the actuality of, both good and evil resides in every human being without exception. Undoubtedly, as I have mentioned earlier in this book and throughout much of my previous writings, we are living at once in overlapping ages: in an original and cosmos-long age of the law of nature and in a subsequent and mankind-long age of the law of reason. Undoubtedly, as a species, we have not yet evolved to that stage when, for the security and benefit not only of ourselves but the totality of life, we can definitively circumvent the potentiality for evil that may be present within each of us.) It will be appropriate now to review what each philosopher has said in his own words.

In *The Analects* (IV. 6), it states:

> The Master said: "I've never seen a person who really loves Humanity and despises Inhumanity. Those who love Humanity know of nothing more essential. And those who despise Inhumanity act with such Humanity that Inhumanity never touches them.
>
> "Can people devote their full strength to Humanity for even a single day? I've never seen anyone who isn't strong enough. There may be such people, but I've never seen them."

In *The Book of Mo Tzu* (at the conclusion of Universal Love, Part III, Section 16), it states:

Now universal love and mutual benefit are both profitable and easy beyond all measure. The only trouble, as I see it, is that no ruler takes any delight in them. If the rulers really delighted in them, promoted them with rewards and praise, and prevented neglect of them by punishments, then I believe that people would turn to universal love and mutual benefit as naturally as fire turns upward or water turns downward, and nothing in the world could stop them.

The principle of universality is the way of the sage kings, the means of bringing safety to the rulers and officials and of assuring ample food and clothing to the people. Therefore the superior man can do no better than to examine it carefully and strive to put it into practice. If he does, then as a ruler he will be generous, as a subject loyal, as a father kind, as a son filial, as an older brother comradely, and as a younger brother respectful. So if the superior man wishes to be a generous ruler, a loyal subject, a kind father, a filial son, a comradely older brother, and a respectful younger brother, he must put into practice this principle of universality. It is the way of the sage kings and a great benefit to the people.

In the West, both Aristotle and, four centuries later, the Roman emperor Marcus Aurelius, championed the moral precept of magnanimity as the supreme, or the most noble, mode of personal conduct. Aristotle contrasts baseness with nobleness: the former moral quality, prevalent among most people and characteristic of the life directed by emotion, pursues self-interest, self-gratification, and self-indulgence in spite of, in precedence of, and at the expense of the satisfaction of the needs of others, and is evil; the latter, prevalent among the few and characteristic of the life directed by reason, seeks to act in the interests of others and, by identifying the satisfaction of one's own needs with the satisfaction of the needs of others, attains the highest sense of self-realization, and is good. For the Stagirite, embracing magnanimity means deciding and acting to put aside and to transcend oneself through self-denial, or even self-sacrifice, for the sake of the well-being, or even the very survival, of others.

Let us further explore the development of his concept of the ethics of magnanimity. In *The Nicomachean Ethics* (Book IX, Chapter VIII), Aristotle writes:

> It is true of the virtuous man that he will act often in the interest of his friends and of his country, and, if need be, will even die for them. He will surrender money, honour, and all the goods for which the world contends, reserving only nobleness for himself, as he would rather en-

joy an intense pleasure for a short time than a moderate pleasure long, and would rather live one year nobly than many years indifferently, and would rather perform one noble and lofty action than many poor actions. This is true of one who lays down his life for another; he chooses great nobleness for his own. Such a man will surrender riches gladly if only he may enrich his friends; for then while his friend gets the money, he gets the nobleness, and so assigns the greater good to himself.

The magnanimity of the Roman sage king, the Stoic philosopher Marcus Aurelius, combines the selflessness of Aristotelian magnanimity with the universality of Confucian and Moist magnanimity. In his *Meditations*, three separate passages (one in Book Five and two in Book Seven) touch on one or the other of these themes.

The first of these passages (5.6) states:

> Some people, when they do someone a favor, are always looking for a chance to call it in. And some aren't, but they're still aware of it—still regard it as a debt. But others don't even do that. They're like a vine that produces grapes without looking for anything in return.
>
> A horse at the end of the race . . .
> A dog when the hunt is over . . .
> A bee with its honey stored . . .
> And a human being after helping others.
>
> They don't make a fuss about it. They just go on to something else, as the vine looks forward to bearing fruit again in season.
>
> We should be like that. Acting almost unconsciously.

The second (7.13) states:

> What is rational in different beings is related, like the individual limbs of a single being, and meant to function as a unit.
>
> This will be clearer to you if you remind yourself: I am a single limb (*melos*) of a larger body—a rational one.
>
> Or you could say "a part" (*meros*)—only a letter's difference. But then you're not really embracing other people. Helping them isn't yet its own reward. You're still seeing it only as The Right Thing To Do. You don't yet realize who you're really helping.

And the third (7.73):

You've given aid and they've received it. And yet, like an idiot, you keep holding out for more: to be credited with a Good Deed, to be repaid in kind. Why?

We should be able to see that the practice of magnanimity is as difficult as it is worthy. It is the optimal expression of goodness. In the words of Aristotle, it is "the crown of the virtues." As a general principle of personal ethics, that conduct which provides the greatest benefits to others demands the greatest self-denial, perhaps even total self-sacrifice. It is for this reason, then, that magnanimity is the select ethics of the few, not the many; of the extraordinary, not the ordinary, human being; of the great, not the small-minded, spirit. As the highest, the most noble, the most self-fulfilling mode of personal conduct that can be adopted, magnanimity is clearly esoteric, essentially individualistic, and not at all social. As altruism, it is also clearly esoteric, essentially individualistic, and not religious. But before we can consider authentic, or personal, magnanimity (altruism), we must first discuss quasi magnanimity (altruism), or social magnanimity and religious altruism.

The defining characteristic of the ethics of magnanimity (as with religious conviction) is personal choice. The practitioners of authentic magnanimity should not be identified with the agents of collective action in behalf of the common well-being. The latter comprise those who serve society within (and, in some situations, afterwards without) established cultural institutions as government leaders, as the aforementioned nurturers of society, and as creative geniuses in the sciences and the arts whose work indirectly contributes to universal knowledge and human self-consciousness. This work of social magnanimity has an obvious value for human well-being and it arises in that level of social awareness that distinguishes fully-developed or advanced civilizations. Nonetheless, we must recognize that those who serve society in the work of social magnanimity are little different from the entrepreneurs and employees who serve both themselves and society through private enterprise. Most people desire and hope to benefit themselves and others through their work. Clearly, that which motivates and, in part, distinguishes those who choose the work of social magnanimity is no more than a desire to attain honor and personal recognition.

The practitioners of authentic magnanimity also should not be identified with the adherents of either of the great altruistic world religions, Mahayana Buddhism and Christianity. The problem of magnanimity in the religions of altruism can be formulated as follows: first, during their lifetimes, magnanimous Christians (or magnanimous Mahayana Buddhists) attempt to provide assistance to others in order to attain a personal benefit after death in the form of salvation (or nirvana); secondly, the metaphysical trains of thought which support this kind of ethical magnanimity are essentially irrational inasmuch as their validity is impossible to confirm within the lifetimes of human beings; thirdly, even if the validity of these trains of thought could be confirmed, religious altruism can not be identified with authentic magnanimity since the ultimate object that provides its motivation is self-interest. Accordingly, religious altruism proceeds from an ignoble deception of the worst kind, as both Nietzsche and Freud have maintained with considerable justice. At once, religious altruism is an hypocrisy, either a willful or an unwitting deception of others, and, for those of whom the hypocrisy may be said to be unintentional, an ignis fatuus, a blind and complete self-deception.

On the other hand, those who adopt the ethics of authentic magnanimity include those who provide a significant benefit to humanity, or to a representative sample thereof, through their own talents and resources, or who perform some personal act to prevent or to relieve a detriment to the same. These persons alone have the ability, desire, and will to practice authentic magnanimity, either in acts of humanitarianism or heroism. These persons can emerge from any segment of society although it appears most likely that numbers in excess of general proportions should emerge from those segments represented by the agents of collective action in behalf of the common well-being or the adherents of the two great altruistic world religions, by virtue of a certain quality and condition—a deeper awareness of human need and a more immediate opportunity to provide service to others—that is prevalent among these groups. Let us take a moment to consider the motivation for such persons, the ones who choose to practice the ethics of magnanimity, whether or not they are actively engaged in work that has obvious social value, and whether or not they are religious.

Stated in the most simple possible terms, magnanimity is a personal recognition of the evil of injury or abuse and a personal desire, fused into resolve and coupled with personal ability, to prevent or to relieve, in an effective and a definitive manner, some concrete instance, or a number of concrete instances, of injury or abuse, whether through independent individual action or extraordinary individual effort within the context of collective action. The ethics of magnanimity, then, arises in a personal obligation, voluntarily assumed, to prevent injury to another, or others, or to relieve the suffering of another, or others. To the extent that some other person, or a group of other persons, should be responsible for causing such injury or abuse, the obligation may be said to be a third party personal obligation. At the same time, it is a unilateral and an internalized obligation (or sense of obligation): it has no legal validity and it can not be recognized by anyone other than the one who has tacitly assumed it. But the problem of injury or abuse has already been addressed by the other ethics of symbiosism: Why should anyone be concerned when one already practices noninjury, when laws are already in place to prohibit injury or abuse, and when one already declines to engage in detrimental reciprocity? Because, for as long as abuse persists or other naturally-caused injury can occur, each of us must care about what happens to each other and, to the extent that we are able, we must remain free to choose to adopt the ethics of magnanimity to relieve suffering or, to the extent that we are able and courageous, we must also remain free to choose to adopt the ethics of magnanimity to arrest or to prevent injury or abuse. Let us proceed to examine in further detail each of the two modes of magnanimity, humanitarianism and heroism, commencing with the latter.

## 1. Heroism

The ethics of noninjury, the ethics of magnanimity, that portion of the ethics of utilitarianism that is concerned with eliminating or controlling the abusive, and the aggregate of those portions of the ethics of reciprocitarianism that condemn detrimental reciprocity and advocate the practices of courtesy, fair play and charity are entirely or largely concerned with preventing or relieving whatever is detrimental to human life and experience. Such detriment may be caused by people or by nonhuman forces of nature. The ethics of noninjury, of course, only addresses detriment caused by people. The ethics of magnanimity, then, applies when the ethics of noninjury fails, when the law under utilitarianism is blind to injustice, or when a detriment otherwise is caused by the forces of nature. We see another person, or a group of people, sustain an injury and we assume a personal obligation to prevent or to relieve it. Why? Because our fundamental personal security requires us to do so. If we do not, then no one would be able to rely on another if and when he or she should happen to sustain an injury. In other words, if we want to be able to expect that anyone will help us if and when we have been injured, we need to be willing to help anyone else who likewise may sometime sustain an injury. However, we may lack an ability to render effective help or, if we are able, we may lack sufficient resolve if we ascertain that we most likely must assume a directly related risk of sustaining injury ourselves; that is, we know that we should act, but we can not, or we will not. But not all of us will fail to act for lack of ability and courage. The ones who can act, and will act, are those who practice the ethics of magnanimity and we are obligated to them inasmuch as they personally assume our obligation in our behalf.

Let us develop this line of thinking a little further. If we should be injured, we could, of course, arrange to pay someone to help us. Only it may be very difficult for us to negotiate such a business transaction during an emergency, or we may lack sufficient financial resources at such a time. In this situation, we must rely upon receiving help as a personal gift. We could promise to reciprocate such help in kind if the person who has helped us should ever sustain an injury in the future but it may be difficult or impossible to honor such a promise without always remaining in close personal contact with that person. Accordingly, our obligation to help others who have been injured is a universal obligation applicable to all human beings and not an arbitrary obligation applicable only to particular people in particular circumstances. Otherwise, we could not realistically expect to receive effective and reliable assistance anytime we should happen to sustain an injury to our person or property. Our personal obligation as a third party to prevent or to relieve an injury sustained by another under the ethics of magnanimity, then, like our obligation to refrain from inflicting injury upon ourselves, or others, or the biosphere under the ethics of noninjury, arises in the concept of justice: what is good for ourselves must necessarily be good for others, and what is good for others must necessarily be good for ourselves. But unlike the practice of the ethics of noninjury, which is easy for anyone to follow without a risk of any harm falling upon the person who practices it, the practice of the ethics of magnanimity generally requires varying degrees of ability and, as it can seldom be practiced in the absence of varying degrees of personal hardship and danger, it requires varying degrees of personal courage. For these reasons, most of us must rely upon those who have a sufficiency of courage and ability to discharge our obligation for us.

The hero is one who has stopped or prevented an injury to another or others. The archetypical hero of Western civilization is Jesus Christ. According to Christian dogma, Jesus serves as a sacrifice in place of a sinful and guilty humanity to absorb the prescribed universal punishment of a just deity: Jesus prevents the injury of damnation. The Christian is obligated to Jesus: the Christian discharges this obligation by following the commandments of Jesus. The appropriate way for us to discharge our obligations to our heroes depends upon the circumstances. If the hero has died in our behalf, our proper response is honor. If not, our response should not be to extend honor, or financial gifts, because such rewards do not comprise the object of heroism: the proper response is to emulate the hero, that is, to follow the example and to respond to the encouragement of our heroes so as to act heroically ourselves in new situations. That failing, for lack of sufficient personal courage and ability, our next best response lies in following the leadership of our heroes in new acts or programs of cooperative action to achieve and to maintain the permanent security and well-being of society.

We must recognize that the role of arresting or preventing injury to human life and experience is the most rudimentary function of government. In this sense, government acts in our behalf to discharge our personal obligation: through government, we can act collectively to meet the objectives that arise under our personal obligation. With an optimal balance of personal freedom and social justice, the fulfillment of this role must become the foremost concern of government once humanity eventually unites under a world democratic federal government. Then, the greatest and the most frequent (although never the only) opportunities for heroism will surely occur in government service. Then, in keeping with Aristotelian ethical and political thought, most of the best of those among us will achieve the greatest possible degree of personal satisfaction, and find the highest possible form of self-realization, through a lifetime of service to mankind in the government of the world democratic state.

## 2. Humanitarianism

The humanitarian is someone who, not lacking a sufficiency of ability and resolve, does something personally to improve the well-being of humanity, or some portion thereof, generally by helping to solve those problems (and to relieve the attendant sufferings) the origins of which can be found in natural disaster, social conflict, sickness, poverty, or ignorance. Unlike the hero, who rises abruptly and courageously on a particular occasion to prevent or to interrupt injury, the humanitarian premeditatedly and solicitously initiates and maintains a process to deal effectively with some specific threat to human survival or well-being. Of course, we can not deny that it is foremost among the valid functions and responsibilities of government at all levels to address all that comprises a detriment or danger to human life and property or otherwise frustrates the efforts of people to take care of themselves adequately. The activities of those who are magnanimous supplement or transcend the activities of government when the activities of government are limited and ineffectual. Accordingly, society should never look only to the operations of government, nor only to the generosity of superior individuals, but to a propitious combination of public activity and private magnanimity to solve the various fundamental problems which may arise to endanger the survival and subsistence of the species.

We can clearly identify two distinct categories of humanitarianism: the donors, who primarily provide substantial financial resources which others can use to relieve the sufferings of humanity, or a specified segment thereof, or suffering of a designated type; and the doers, who singularly provide a unique benefit to relieve human suffering within a particular category or to initiate a significant and lasting social reform.

In the first category, we can include those humanitarians who donate sufficient financial support to carry out specific objectives to provide an obvious benefit for the general public, whether of the world as a whole; the population of a particular nation, region, or city; or the potential victim-beneficiaries within a specified category of abuse, misfortune, or deprivation. Examples of such humanitarians include Alfred Nobel, the Swedish inventor of dynamite who amassed a fortune during his lifetime from the manufacture and sale of explosives and who left more than nine million dollars upon his death to finance a series of cash prizes to reward persons who make outstanding contributions for the benefit of mankind in various fields, including physiology/medicine, physics, literature, chemistry, peace, and economics; Andrew Carnegie, the American iron and steel manufacturer of Scottish descent who accumulated more than 275 million dollars over his business career, donating much of this fortune to create endowments for cultural and educational institutions and foundations, including funds to build 2,800 free public libraries; and John D. Rockefeller, the American industrialist who amassed a personal fortune of one billion dollars from his business interests in petroleum, railroads, iron and steel, and other industries, and donated 600 million dollars to create endowments for educational, agricultural research, and medical research foundations, including 183 million dollars for one, the Rockefeller Foundation, organized "to promote the well-being of mankind throughout the world."

In the second category, we can include those humanitarians who, having become poignantly conscious of some particular source of human suffering, resolve to relieve such suffering, and even to attempt to eliminate the very source of such suffering, through personal effort and leadership. Examples of this kind of humanitarianism include Jean Henri Dunant, the Swiss entrepreneur who, in the course of arranging a personal meeting with Napoleon III (for the purpose of acquiring certain water rights) at a time when the latter was on military campaign against the Austrians, witnessed the savage carnage of the Battle of Solferino in Lombardy, an impression which motivated Dunant to propose and to found the Red Cross (in 1863) and to provide leadership in organizing and establishing the first Geneva Convention (in 1864)—a worldwide institution and an international agreement which together serve to assist and to protect the sick and the wounded of armies during wartime; Albert Schweitzer, the Alsatian-German Renaissance man who, after winning recognition as a great performing artist (organist) and a major scholar and author in various disciplines (music, theology, and philosophy), took a degree in medicine and moved to French Equatorial Africa (now Gabon, Africa), where he established a hospital at Lambaréné (in 1913) and devoted the remainder of his life to minister to the sick among one of the most primitive societies in the world; and Peter Benenson, the British lawyer of English and Russian-Jewish descent who, reacting to a newspaper story of an incident in which two students were imprisoned in Portugal for raising a toast to liberty, founded Amnesty International (in 1961) to foster a general awareness of the hopeless and dismal situation of persons who have been unjustly imprisoned (because of their race or ethnic origin, or their political or religious convictions), to provide encouragement and support for such persons and their families, and to assist in gaining their immediate or eventual release.

Until the inauguration of a world democratic federal government and for a considerable period of time thereafter until its eventual coming-of-age, there will persist an enormous need for the practice of humanitarianism by concerned individuals since the greater portion of the population of the world continues to live in ignorance, sickness, and poverty under conditions that remain unhealthy, unsanitary, and dangerous. It will not be enough if all people in the world refrain from committing acts of violence and injury, engage in useful activity while tolerating apparent uselessness and eschewing abuse, and initiate beneficial behavior toward others or engage in beneficial reciprocity while eschewing detrimental reciprocity: too many people—the unfortunate, the disadvantaged, the underprivileged—remain subject to laws of nature that have not as yet been amended through the power of reason. Only a combination of the practice of humanitarianism by private parties and the implementation of public policy to maintain and to improve the environment of society will suffice to ensure the permanent security and well-being of humanity.

As with the practice of heroism, the practice of the doer form of humanitarianism originates in opportunity, that is, at the intersection of awareness, concern, and resolve. For the donor form, of course, personal ability must also be present. Before the advent of modern history, only the members of the upper classes could be magnanimous. Today, wherever feudalism, imperialism, totalitarianism, and communism have been supplanted by democracy, and societal stratification by egalitarianism, anyone can be, or can eventually come to be, magnanimous.

Let us then conclude our presentation of the ethics of magnanimity by posing this candid question: "And who should practice magnanimity?"

Our only possible response: "Only those who are suited should practice magnanimity, and each person must decide for himself, or herself, whether he, or she, is truly capable of embracing magnanimity, since magnanimity is like a pair of shoes of a certain size and style—let those wear the shoes for whom the shoes fit."

# Synthesis

Throughout the course of this book, I have attempted to introduce the philosophy of symbiosism, a composite morality which will be suitable and effective to enable all human beings in all places to live together as a unified species under one common democratic government. At once, this philosophy will serve to provide a secure foundation for public laws, social mores, and personal values. It will serve to establish a compelling rationale for the draft and ratification of a universal social contract. It will serve to determine and, consequently, to justify the policies and operations of government at all levels and the plans and activities of individuals within all dimensions of human conduct. The philosophy of symbiosism will be suitable for general use by all people because it is predicated upon reason, that mental faculty that, in the fullness of its potentiality and actuality, is common to all people and that functions to bind all people together. It will be effective for the same reason, inasmuch as reason is that unique instrumentality that enables mankind to solve the problems of survival and to optimize the enjoyment of life.

Today, we live at once in the age of the law of nature and the parallel age of the law of reason. The latter commenced a little more than three hundred years ago, after the Renaissance and during the Scientific Revolution in Europe, more specifically in or around 1690 with the publication in England of Isaac Newton's *Principia* and John Locke's *Essay Concerning Human Understanding* and *Two Treatises of Government*. The essential features that distinguish the events of the age of the law of reason throughout the entire world include, on the one hand, the ascendence of scientific technology and, on the other, a new and growing human self-consciousness, a general understanding that more similarities than differences are observable between human beings, a universal understanding that all people everywhere are members of a single species who share common needs, interests, and desires. Since the onset of the more recent of these two trains of events, they have increasingly progressed in tandem so that, at the present, they imply the sociopolitical unification of mankind through the inauguration of a world democratic federal government in the very near future.

The moral foundation for such a unified world can be nothing other than the philosophy of symbiosism or some similar composite morality that would likewise be predicated upon reason although it should be designated by a completely different name. The moral foundation for a unified world can never be the ethics of a religion or the combined ethics of a number of religions since this kind of ethics has its foundation in religion, which in turn primarily arises from the mental processes of the mental faculty of emotion and not from that of reason. Furthermore, no single religion is common to all people and no rational foundation has ever been established to support a definitive argument that any particular religion should be. Since the present, as well as the initial, purpose of religion must be seen as an attempt to enable mankind to withstand or to overcome the forces of nature and to live together without inflicting injury upon each other, and since the sole responsibility for the satisfactory performance of both of these functions has recently been, and presently continues to be, primarily entrusted to reason, we can expect that religion itself must ultimately become obsolete (under the promising and probable assumption that the lives of all, or of at least most, people will ultimately be governed by reason and not by emotion) at some point in the distant future. We can also expect that the current major world religions will not entirely disappear, but will persist as mythologies and, ultimately, mankind most likely will discover certain truths about itself through the continuing study of such mythologies, even as it so does in the present through the study of the mythologies of the ancient world or of primitive societies.

I would like to digress briefly at this point to offer some comments with respect to the future of philosophy. At the time of Aristotle, almost all that we could know, or could attempt to understand—certainly, all that we would call "advanced knowledge"—was included within the realm of philosophy. Wherever the validity of an assertion was neither self-evident nor ever demonstrable through sensory experience, it was affirmed or denied exclusively through the operations of the methodology of logic. Wherever logic was permitted to work with unproven propositions or false assumptions, its conclusions, of course, would also then be subject to question. Wherever propositions could be proven or otherwise accepted with a high degree of probability, the relevant body of knowledge could, and would, be released from philosophy to establish or to enrich a particular sphere of knowledge within the general organization of phenomena, which is to say, that it would be relegated to a distinct science. Additional knowledge would be admitted to each science once the underlying assertions could be validated through the evidence derived from sensory experience over the course of numerous trials. Definitive knowledge, then, depended upon a two-stage process—theoretical speculation and experiential confirmation. Today, all of the recognized sciences include some portion of knowledge that is derived from theoretical speculation but which remains inadmissible, and therefore temporarily suspended, as it were, until the validity of the underlying assertions can be demonstrated to the senses through an active process of objective testing. Today, all that remain in philosophy are the three branches of epistemology, ethics and aesthetics.

Epistemology is directly concerned with the examination of human knowledge. Among the great philosophers of ancient Greece, Aristotle stood closest to that position that recognizes that theoretical speculation in and of itself is inadequate to provide knowledge that is fully valid or that can otherwise be relied upon with a great degree of confidence. The requirement that the validity of the conclusions of theoretical speculation be confirmed by means of objective sensory experience acquired in the course of a deliberate process of methodical testing emerged from that line of Western philosophy that originated with Aristotle but developed and flourished within the philosophical tradition of Great Britain (most notably through the work of Francis Bacon and John Locke) and that is commonly designated by the term "empiricism." With the ascendence of empiricism, the epistemological controversy has finally been resolved. We can acknowledge that theoretical speculation is generally necessary but always insufficient and therefore dependent upon something else within any rational process for the discovery of knowledge. Epistemology, then, need no longer occupy a position among the concerns of philosophy in the future.

During the course of the previous century, both logic and metaphysics have largely, if not entirely, migrated from philosophy to science. Metaphysics is concerned with the examination of reality, and the examination of reality distinguishes two distinct categories of inquiry—the objective (that is, the physical universe, or cosmology) and the subjective (that is, conscious being, or ontology). The first category has long since been relegated to the various physical sciences. The second can certainly be relegated to relevant categories among the infant social sciences and, in particular, should comprise an appropriate, discrete, and composite or synthetic division within the science of psychology. Under this reformulation, we would no longer read Heidegger's *Being and Time* or Sartre's *Being and Nothingness* as philosophy but as theoretical psychology.

Aesthetics can similarly be considered as a branch of psychology. Since ethics largely (although not exclusively) involves interpersonal behavior, we can presently neither relegate it fully to psychology nor to sociology and inasmuch as the infant social science of anthropology is primarily concerned at present with prehistoric man or primitive cultures, it does not yet appear to be an appropriate discipline for the immediate exposition and future development of ethics. Nevertheless, with a growing recognition of the need for one science to encompass contemporary man with all aspects of his interpersonal relationships, we can expect that such a science will quickly emerge—perhaps as a mature and refined form or division of the infant science of anthropology; perhaps as a synthesis of psychology and sociology or of psychology, sociology, and anthropology; or perhaps even as an entirely new social science unrelated to any other—into which we will be able to relegate the last remaining branch of philosophy. Then, like religion, philosophy will become obsolete, fulfilling no significant function other than providing an historical narrative of the intellectual interests and values of early man.

The philosophy of symbiosism includes four components, three of which are crucial for personal and social well-being and the fourth of which is crucial for complementing or perfecting one or another of the first three in certain emergencies or persisting dangerous situations where their efficaciousness is irrelevant, untapped, or inadequate. In the order of ethical priority, the order of their previous introduction and development, the four components include the ethics of noninjury, utilitarianism, reciprocitarianism, and the ethics of magnanimity. As we have said, the ethics of noninjury enjoins each person to refrain from inflicting injury upon any person, including oneself, or upon any other form of sentient or beneficial life. Utilitarianism enjoins each person, whether he or she is acting alone or in concert with others, to pursue that which is useful, to eschew all that which is abusive, and to maintain an impartial and unflagging tolerance for whatever appears to be useless, so long as it can be determined that such activity neither contributes to, nor leads to, abuse. Reciprocitarianism enjoins each person to behave toward other people in such a manner as may be most likely to elicit beneficial reciprocity. Such initiatory behavior is instrumental in preventing ill will or misunderstanding and in creating friendship and love. Magnanimity enjoins each person, to the extent that he or she may be able and willing, to save others heroically in times of crisis and to correct or to mitigate some detrimental condition in society or the biosphere through extraordinary personal generosity or leadership. Each of the four ethical components of symbiosism is directly connected with each of the others in promoting the prevention, avoidance, or mitigation of injury to human beings or, indeed, to all other forms of sentient or beneficial life, irrespective of the form or the cause of the injury. Utilitarianism and reciprocitarianism are additionally connected with each other in promoting the acquisition of the means to satisfy human needs and, consequently, to engender lasting human happiness. Let us now recapitulate the ethics of symbiosism by restating its components as an indivisible composite in the order of ethical priority, beginning with a terse reformulation of the aggregate of tenets that address the prevention or correction of all of that which is detrimental to human life or its environment.

As has been the first principle of medicine since the time of Hippocrates, so the first principle of ethics for as long as the human species endures must be "First, do no harm." We would argue that the meaning of life for any given person derives from that person's experience in satisfying the necessities of life while averting or enduring the hurts of life. Accordingly, every person desires to survive and to enjoy life. Now, rights and obligations arise in social experience, so, to the extent that each person is willing to accept a personal obligation as the corollary of a personal right, we can say that each person has a personal right to live, to be free, and to attempt to enjoy life without being infringed upon, interfered with, or harmed by any other person, provided that that same person accept a personal obligation not to infringe upon, to interfere with, or to harm any other person. The rationale in support of this personal right and personal obligation, including the interrelationship between the right and the obligation, should be self-evident through the recognition of the formation of a moral contract. This is the first of three discrete moral unions of personal right with personal obligation (that is, the first of three inferred interpersonal moral contracts) which are critical for human happiness, although unexpressed, and which we will consider under symbiosism.

Our moral agreement not to harm others must be broad enough to preclude any kind of injury unintentionally inflicted upon others through our acts of negligence or even of recklessness. Furthermore, in any situation where we may be induced or coerced by some third party to inflict intentional injury upon another, we must, of course, repudiate such an inducement or disengage from such a coercion—in the latter instance, either through heroic resistance or unequivocal withdrawal (if necessary, even flight).

In one of its three fundamental evaluative assertions, utilitarianism, like the ethics of noninjury, condemns abusive activity. We can say that a correct, albeit an incomplete, expression of the principle of utility is the assertion that that action is best which prevents or decreases unhappiness for the greatest number. We can also say that utilitarianism informs us, at least in part, to do the things which will enable us to eliminate or to mitigate the sufferings of life.

To the extent that any person violates the personal ethics of noninjury, which is at once so simple and rational, so appropriate and effectual for protecting all people of the world through common understanding and voluntary compliance (which is to say, that such a person enjoys one's personal right without honoring one's personal obligation under the most fundamental of moral contracts), and consequently fails to refrain from inflicting injury upon others, whether by deliberate act, negligence, recklessness, or coercion, then any effort to correct or to control abusive behavior must become a societal or public venture, appropriately falling under the ethics of utilitarianism. This arena of human endeavor, wherein a person engages in useful activity (in concert with other like-minded persons) to prevent or to minimize a detriment to the greatest number, embraces the professions and occupations of medicine, law, and social work in addition to the most fundamental operations of democratic government. Accordingly, the effort to prevent all that is detrimental becomes at once a personal initiative and a social objective. In the latter instance, the commission of crimes and torts is effectively deterred through the enactment and enforcement of legislation.

The cardinal mechanism to provide protection against injury for humanity, for all other sentient beings, and for the biosphere itself, will emerge in the near future upon the inauguration of a universal democratic federal government and the consequential establishment of binding universal law, the heart of which must be a universal social contract, featuring the immediate and irrevocable criminalization and prohibition of war. Binding universal law, of course, will also need to include comprehensive and effectual environmental legislation within and between all jurisdictions of the world government. No other single measure will do so much to relieve, and ultimately to do away with, the perennial and ubiquitous sufferings of mankind.

Today, we are living in an era of national democratization, when many of the remaining oligarchies of the world are gradually or abruptly transforming into democracies, and when many of the embryonic democracies are slowly taking on more and more of the essential features of democratic government. This process of national democratization will surely continue after the process of world federalization has begun and the two political processes will likely run concurrently for a long time as many of the world's national democracies join the world democratic federation. Ultimately, most of the remaining oligarchies of the world will become democratic, and most of the democracies will become members of the world democratic federal government.

Now, we have previously identified a number of insidious practices of desensitization which have persisted through the onset of the age of the law of reason as a kind of archaic residual from an age when human beings relied upon brute strength and interpersonal intimidation to satisfy the necessities of life. These practices include the various forms of prejudice and xenophobia that emerge during the course of interpersonal discrimination; dehumanization of the enemy during military training; hazing; hunting; and the activities of those sports that feature cruelty, such as in fights between human beings, between animals, or between human beings and animals, that are commercially arranged as entertainments for insensate spectators. Since all of these practices are virtually obsolete, and since they clearly violate all of those principles which together form the very heart of symbiosism, we must propose that legislation be introduced in every society on earth to abolish all of these practices for good.

To the extent that science may be able to provide definitive proof that some portion of our behavior originates in instinct, and until it may be able to offer a better method for us to manage any detrimental consequences of such instinctive behavior, we may need to counteract our unconscious aggression through acts of sublimation, whereby we determinedly confront our fears and anger and consciously occupy ourselves with constructive and beneficial projects.

Furthermore, we will always need to continue to manage the consequences of our behavior, whenever it is detrimental to others and/or to ourselves, by exercising self-discipline through moderation in the experience of sensual pleasure, whether in the enjoyment of eating, of drinking alcoholic beverages, or of sexual gratification.

With respect to the issue of suicide, we must hold that any act of suicide, including any unsuccessful act of attempted suicide, can never be justified except under either of two circumstances. The first involves sociopolitical activism under oligarchy where no other means are present to allow an expression of outrage against grave injustice. The second involves euthanasia for persons dying with unbearable and unassuageable physical pain during the course of terminal illness. In the first case, once

the sociopolitical processes of national democratization and world federalization have been completed, oligarchy will disappear and with it the
need and justification for suicidal sociopolitical activism. As for the issue
of euthanasia, we would urge that the decision to practice euthanasia always be offered as an option in given situations involving a patient's unbearable and unassuageable suffering where the hopelessness of his or
her medical prognosis is certain.

Reciprocitarianism is that form of ethics, of a personal ethics,
wherein, among other things, each of us endeavors to act towards others
in a manner that is intended to establish or to maintain adequate safeguards against as many as may be possible of the myriad hurts of life,
specifically those hurts the origins of which can clearly be traced to ma-
licious behavior arising from ill will. Under reciprocitarianism, we at
once repudiate malevolence and maleficence and embrace benevolence
and beneficence. Likewise, we repudiate detrimental reciprocity, or retaliation, and we seek at best only to secure reparation for our injury and
loss through the operation of justice under the law. We achieve our objectives under reciprocitarianism in a number of ways: by our not holding ill will for others and by our effective communicating of this private
position; by our holding goodwill for others and by our effective communicating of the same; by our practice of courtesy as the most essential
quality of rational interpersonal communication; by our practice of fair
play in all of our interpersonal dealings; and by our practice of charity
wherever it is needed, to the extent that we are able.

The bipartite function of the practice of courtesy is not only to reveal
the presence of goodwill but to reveal the absence of ill will. Any effort
to practice courtesy is, in part, an attempt to prevent maleficence, by attempting to prevent any instance of effrontery or personal disregard that
might then be interpreted as a kind of detrimental initiatory behavior,
however minute or ambiguous, and that might give rise to an act of detrimental reciprocity, thereby setting in motion a recurring cycle of malevolence and maleficence.

We have said that the practice of courtesy precipitates the initial and
most fundamental catalysis of interpersonal harmony. Since the practice
of courtesy creates this kind of effect in our communications and dealings with one another, the teaching of courtesy needs to become a major
priority in the moral training of the young along with education in the
ethics of noninjury and the fundamental psychosocial and biospheric
concepts of equity.

The cardinal function of public education in the common society of a
world unified under one universal democratic federal government must

be to provide universal training in the ethics of noninjury and the related concepts and practices of courtesy and fair play. As we have said, once the children and the young people of the world have been raised to understand and to practice the ethics of noninjury, courtesy, and fair play, human society will gradually become transformed in such a manner as to insure and to increase personal security, prosperity, and happiness everywhere.

We have further said that we must extend universal public moral education beyond the periods of childhood and adolescence for all of those persons who have been convicted of crime. This form of continuing education must occur during the period of the sentence, that is, during the period of incarceration, when the convict is experiencing rehabilitation for eventual reentry into society, so that all convicts will be given every opportunity to come to accept full responsibility for their personal behavior, to learn from their past mistakes, and ultimately to go forth to avail themselves of a new opportunity to seek, and hopefully to find, happiness in their lives without causing further injury to themselves, to others, or to the physical and societal environments.

We have talked at length about the reciprocity between unequals in a democratic society. The nurturers of society—the educators, the physicians and the various other providers of health care, and the law enforcement officials and the various other rehabilitators of convicted criminals—must come to receive both the highest financial rewards and the highest honors of society, inasmuch as everyone receives indispensable and irreplaceable benefits, both as individuals and as members of society, from their efforts.

The sovereign maxim of ethics is the principle of noninjury with its inherent reciprocity of personal right and personal obligation. This maxim provides the foundation for the concept of justice and the practice of fair play. Wherever injustice can not be corrected by the operation of law, each person assumes a personal obligation to oppose such injustice, to neutralize its effects, to call public attention to it, and to lobby for the introduction of new legislation to eradicate it. This is the second of three inferred (although they are unexpressed) interpersonal moral contracts. If I can enjoy a personal right to be treated fairly by others—without prejudice either for my position within any of the various categories of society or any particular weakness or misfortune of my life—then I must assume a personal obligation to uphold justice or, conversely, and of greater importance, to oppose and to attempt to eliminate injustice in all of its forms. We may confidently assert, then, that wherever utilitarianism may not yet be adequate to establish or to maintain justice, we must rely upon

reciprocitarianism (and, to a lesser extent, the ethics of magnanimity) to
lead the moral fight against injustice.

Through acts of charity or magnanimity, a person may attempt to
prevent injury to, or to relieve suffering of, another person, or a number
of persons, sometimes in conjunction with the collective efforts of society (through governmental operations) toward the same ends. The ethics
of noninjury requires that every person assume a personal obligation not
to cause injury. Wherever injury arises, either because of one's failure to
honor one's personal obligation or from some cause other than one that is
human, every person assumes a new personal obligation—whether as
one arising from the practice of fair play under reciprocitarianism or as
another from participation in the social contract under utilitarianism or as
still another to assist people in distress by means of an act of charity under reciprocitarianism or an act of heroism under the ethics of magnanimity—to attempt to prevent, to stop, or to relieve the consequences of
such an injury, as the case may be, both in an effort as an individual
(whether acting by oneself or through cooperation with others) and in an
effort as a member of society, that is, as a citizen of a nation within the
world community and as a potential citizen of the coming world democratic state. All efforts beyond the practice of the ethics of noninjury to
prevent or to control injury to all forms of sentient and beneficial life will
surely require a combination of individual initiatives and governmental
operations to achieve optimal success. We can confidently acknowledge
that wherever the ethics of noninjury in and of itself may seem to fail
altogether, its essential tenets are so fundamental to each of the remaining ethics of symbiosism that utilitarianism, reciprocitarianism, and the
ethics of magnanimity will be able to operate both singly and in concert
to prevent or to control injury to the members of the human species, to
all other sentient and beneficial life forms, and to the entire biosphere of
the earth.

With respect to the issue of humaneness, which we acknowledge to
be central to the practice of the ethics of noninjury, we further acknowledge that compassion for all forms of sentient life creates a double benefit: first, compassion between human beings generally increases as compassion is extended to all sentient beings (affording the broadest and the
most fundamental application of reciprocitarianism) and, second, those
lower species of animals which, like human beings, are conscious to
some degree of a sensation of pain during the experience of an injury
will be effectively protected against all needless and unjustified suffering
caused by human beings. Ultimately, we will need to rely upon the science of biology to inform us as to the extent to which we must descend

the phylogenetic tree in extending our compassion over the entire range of sentient beings. At the present, we will certainly do well in mounting this effort if we begin to give up eating meat, wearing fur apparel, and hunting animals for recreation. We will certainly do best to condemn all forms of cruelty to animals, including the abuse of animals in such cruel sports as bullfights, dogfights, cockfights, and the like. We will also do best to support current advances in medical science and biotechnology so that the use and consequent sufferings of animals in the service of medical research will come to a permanent end as quickly as possible.

With respect to the issue of environmentalism, which creates a benefit not only in behalf of all human beings, or of all sentient beings, but of the entire biosphere upon which all life is dependent, our interest will be focused upon three areas: natural catastrophe prediction, antipollution, and conservation. All of these comprise the fundamental branches of environmentalism and each one requires the active involvement of government at all levels inasmuch as the very survival and ultimate well-being of all human life depends upon a viable natural environment. The necessity for accurate and timely natural catastrophe prediction and for broad and effective antipollution and conservation measures is already incontrovertibly self-evident. Ultimately, we will need to rely upon the science of ecology to inform us as to the identity of the precise species that are directly or indirectly beneficial for human survival and well-being, the optimal numbers of such species, and the optimal ratios between the same to maintain a natural equilibrium and to avoid a natural disaster. At the present, we should do well to maintain zoos and botanical gardens in our urban centers with wilderness sanctuaries for both flora and fauna in all outlying areas; to prohibit or to restrict the killing or capture of individuals within any endangered species; and to prohibit or to restrict the destruction of natural habitats in the residential, commercial, or industrial development of privately-owned lands or in the construction, maintenance, or expansion of public infrastructure. To the extent that we should choose to ignore or to depreciate conservation, we will permit incalculable and irreparable harm eventually to befall our progeny.

We have suggested that the ethics of magnanimity is an esoteric ethics, an ethics for those today who are most like those in ancient times who Confucius referred to as "the noble-minded," the ethics of a moral elite. However, even as humaneness is central to the ethics of noninjury and, through a posture of goodwill and the practice of courtesy, fair play, and charity, the most fundamental application of reciprocitarianism, so it is also, through the demonstration of mercy or the act of heroism, the most rudimentary application of the ethics of magnanimity. Let us note that all of these expressions of humaneness have a negative aspect, such that the one who is humane refrains from inflicting injury upon other sentient beings (even in circumstances sanctioning justifiable retribution), and some of the same expressions also have a positive aspect, such that the one who is humane helps other sentient beings who, or that, have been injured or threatened with an exposure to injury (whether by a third party or through natural causes), either at the moment of injury (by attempting to prevent it) or afterwards (by attempting to relieve suffering and perhaps to save lives). This dual aspect of humaneness is also present in the ethics of magnanimity, where the positive aspect finds expression in auxiliary humaneness, the ethics of the good shepherd, the smallest, simplest, most fundamental expression of heroism. This expression of humaneness under either reciprocitarianism or the ethics of magnanimity gives rise to the third of three inferred interpersonal moral contracts: every person has a personal obligation to help others who may be suffering an injury and every person has a personal right to expect that others will provide help if he or she may be suffering an injury. To the extent that a person lacks sufficient courage to act heroically, he or she must rely upon others to discharge the obligation in his or her behalf. Then the person who lacks courage must attempt to emulate his or her hero models in new situations, whether by performing acts of heroism single-handedly in proportion to the magnitude of one's courage or by performing the same in concert with others, thereby finding comfort in, and drawing support from, mutual encouragement and collective strength.

Since the foremost function of government is to provide security for the members of society, both individually and collectively, we can expect that the greatest and most frequent opportunities for the expression of heroism will arise in the service of the coming world democratic federal government.

In the course of our discussion, we discerned that there is always a kind of no-man's-land between good and evil in which human activity can be seen to be neither good nor evil but merely useless. For some, useless activity is usually inferred to be evil under a criterion that rejects any human activity that obviously does not create an immediate or timely benefit as a waste of time and a detraction from goodness. For others, useless activity is usually inferred to be good under a criterion that accepts any human activity that obviously does not create an immediate or timely benefit as either a kind of personal restorative activity or an activity that may eventually create a benefit which might otherwise never oc-

cur. Examples of the former determination include eating, sleeping, rest-
ing after work, entertainment, recreation, holiday and vacation activities,
recuperation from illness or physical injury, and similar diversionary and
recuperative activities. Examples of the latter include education, scholar-
ship, academic and industrial research and development, technological
invention, and similar progressive and creative endeavors. In either instance, continuing popular toleration of apparently useless activity will
require unfailing personal judiciousness to prevent unaccountability, injustice, and abuse. Unless abuse becomes apparent, the various kinds of
apparently useless activity should be tolerated and perhaps even encouraged inasmuch as they provide unquestionable benefits for all human
beings, individually and/or collectively as the kind of activity may be.

With respect to situations involving artistic activity or religious practice, we must offer a few additional comments.

We have asserted that the experience of beauty, whether it should be
present to us in nature or in art, is a vicarious experience for that of satisfying one's needs or of preventing, avoiding, or mitigating one's hurts.
We are not saying that the experience of beauty is the same as the experience of satisfying a need or of attaining security from harm, of
course, but only that the experience of beauty serves as a symbol for the
satisfaction of our needs or for protection against dangers and liberation
from harm. Since the experience of beauty neither facilitates nor hinders
our efforts to satisfy our needs and to mitigate our hurts, since our effective efforts to satisfy our needs and to mitigate our hurts naturally provides us our primary source of pleasure and happiness, and since our experience of beauty rationally provides us an additional source of pleasure
and happiness such that our experience of pleasure and happiness increases, we must conclude that our experience of beauty is generally
beneficial. Wherever the activities of the performing arts provide us an
experience of beauty, such activities are clearly useful. Whenever the
activities of the creative arts may provide us a potential for the experience of beauty, such activities, while apparently useless in the present,
should be tolerated and perhaps even encouraged, so long as there remains a future possibility for consequential benefit with no future possibility for consequential harm.

It has also been our desire and intent to attempt to provide some salient observations with respect to contemporary religious practice
throughout the world. We have endeavored to establish two facts. One,
which is relevant for the religions of monotheism and, by extension, to
all other religions which rely upon a belief in supernatural beings and/or
supernatural states:  neither the existence nor the nonexistence of God

can be proved. The evidence which we have acquired to the present of the process of natural evolution—the long-standing presence of inorganic matter prior to the origin of life and the apparent natural progression through time from the simple and primordial to the complex and mature—suggest a cause of the origin of natural evolution other than that of divine intelligence. God, or the concept of God, then, most likely is a creation of the human imagination—a symbol of perfection, of all that is attainable in human knowledge, and of an ideal for all that is perfectible in human conduct—a concept presently plausible not so much as the indisputable first cause of natural evolution as a possible and desirable ultimate objective of the same. A full development of this proposition is well beyond the scope of this work and it may be taken up, along with a discussion of symbolism in art, as the essential content of an independent creative effort at a future time. Two, the inferable consequences of religious practice are jumbled in ambiguity. On the one hand, religious experience appears to relieve personal anxiety; to provide each believer a direction for life, a model for personal conduct, and a meaning for death; and to increase personal happiness. In addition, religious ethics in general appear to be beneficial for human society, at least where the consensus can attest that they serve as an effective and appropriate guide for interpersonal conduct at at least the most rudimentary levels of social behavior. On the other hand, religious practice clearly creates a number of insuperable social problems:  religious warfare, social divisiveness, and psychological dependence. Since some of the consequences of religious practice are beneficial while others are detrimental, such that the effects of certain kinds of religious practice are neutralized by those of others, we have initially included religious practice among activities that appear to be useless. As such, they may continue to be tolerated like any other forms of restorative or diversionary activities (such as entertainment and recreation), so long as they obviously are not abusive. This means, first, that religious practice can never be tolerated wherever it openly promotes or condones crime or injustice, wherever such crime or injustice may be perpetuated. Accordingly, Islamic practices must not only be conspicuously rejected but vehemently condemned as rank abuse of generally tolerative religious practice and as noxious crimes against humanity wherever they include or promote jihad, terrorism, and malevolence against non-Muslims. This means, secondly, that religious practice can never be tolerated in the political arena of a democratic society. Religious practice and political activity must always remain separated under democracy since the politics of a well-founded society must necessarily be fully predicated upon reason, whereas religious ethics are generally predicated upon a metaphysics that can neither be affirmed nor disaffirmed through reason. This means, thirdly, that religious practice can never be tolerated wherever it prohibits, discourages, or otherwise precludes the believer's full exercise of his or her reason or wherever it refuses to acknowledge the validity of rational conclusions or the plausibility of probable hypotheses.

To conclude our summary of that portion of the ethics of symbiosism that addresses abuse and uselessness, let us posit that we must hate nothing but hate itself, until hate no longer occurs among human beings. We must hate no one except one who hates, and even then, we must endeavor to understand the cause of that one's hatred in order to eliminate it. Likewise, we must be intolerant of nothing but of abuse and of intolerance itself (except, of course, for intolerance of abuse) until abuse and intolerance are eliminated altogether. We must remain intolerant of no one except of one who hates or of one who is intolerant (except for one who is intolerant of abuse) and even then, we must endeavor to understand the cause of that one's hatred or intolerance in order to abolish it for the remainder of human existence and for the permanent well-being of the human species.

Now let us return to those aspects of two of the four ethical components of symbiosism, of utilitarianism and reciprocitarianism, that are interconnected in promoting all that is useful and beneficial for human survival and well-being. Utilitarianism is highly objective—and essentially a social ethics; reciprocitarianism, highly subjective—and essentially a personal ethics. These two moral philosophies are analogous and complementary, one promoting social cohesion and ecological compatibility, the other, interpersonal intercourse and personal happiness. The ethics of symbiosism requires and employs an amalgamation of objectivism and subjectivism to create, at any given time, the optimal human condition, whether for the species as a whole or for any of its discrete individuals. If a universal ethics must serve to satisfy, or to help to satisfy, the needs of each person as well as those of the entire human community and its various subcommunities, that ethics at once must be objective and subjective: objective—to access, unify, and benefit all of mankind through the universal exercise of the faculty of reason; subjective—to involve, liberate, and open a possibility for happiness to each person through the mode of informed self-expression. Embracing objectivity, symbiosism can be practiced in common by every human being; embracing subjectivity, it can permit a distinct, or even a unique, experience, or set of experiences, for each person.

Utilitarianism is predicated upon a principle that validates useful activity by individuals and groups, that asserts that that action is best that creates or increases the happiness of the greatest number (meaning, by extension and by inference, the well-being of all of mankind), and that identifies useful activities as those which enable us to satisfy the needs of life. Utilitarianism enables human beings to identify those plans and courses of action that will be optimal for the satisfaction of human needs. Notwithstanding acts of magnanimity, we may conclude that utilitarianism is primarily a social ethics, one that essentially applies to groups, associations, corporations, and governments. Utilitarianism must also be recognized as the fountainhead of two practical and complementary ideologies (within the joint context of which it generally functions effectually): the political ideology of democracy and the economic ideology of free-fair capitalism. The latter requires the former, and the social contract embodies the organizing principle of the former.

The social contract is an agreement between each person and the remaining members of his or her society to provide, through mutual activity, personal security and various other general benefits that could not otherwise be reliably realized except through a cooperative effort under such an agreement. Personal security is provided through the establishment and enforcement of criminal law. Other common benefits include such policies and procedures as educating the young, underwriting insurance against personal losses arising from disability and natural disaster, providing subsistent retirement income for the elderly, protecting the natural environment, building and repairing the infrastructure, and regulating the economy. The social contract finds expression in the national constitution and in all other laws at each tier of government within the nation. Once the democratic nations of the world unite under a world democratic federation, the social contract will be uniform for all of the citizens within the jurisdictions of the world government. Then, the social contract will find expression in the world constitution and in all other laws at each tier of government within the world federation. The laws which ensure personal security must also provide justice throughout society while protecting the personal freedoms of its members. The ultimate function of the social contract must be to express an effective reconciliation of any conflicts between freedom and justice.

Under the legal principle of quasi contract, no citizen of a democratic nation, having once received, accepted, and enjoyed the benefits of the social contract of his or her society, regardless of whether at a time prior or subsequent to the inauguration of the world democratic federal government, can refuse to be bound by it.

The social contract establishes democracy and authorizes democratic government. Democracy is the optimal political expression of utilitarianism. Since democracy is that form of government in which political power is held by the people (and is exercised by the people either directly or through elected representatives and their agents), democracy independently gives rise to such activities which create benefits, or prevent detriments, for the greatest number. All other expressions of utilitarianism are largely, if not exclusively, dependent upon the principles, policies, and operations of democratic government.

Under democracy, the government is charged with the responsibility of enforcing the social contract. Accordingly, it must defend freedom and promote justice. The fair requirements of democratic government include introducing principles and measures to establish universal suffrage, majority rule, and an effective crosshatch diffusion of political authority. The free requirements of democratic government include introducing principles and measures to provide for, or to support, freedom of conscience, religious freedom, religious toleration, separation of church and state, separation of religion and politics, free access to relevant information, academic freedom, freedom of speech, freedom of the press, an informed citizenry, public debate of political issues, the party system, and protection of individual and minority rights.

Free-fair capitalism is fully dependent upon democracy. It is the optimal economic expression of utilitarianism. Since free-fair capitalism is that form of economic system in which economic power is held by the people (and exercised by the people either directly or through corporations and similar organizations, including government), free-fair capitalism provides financial and economic benefits, or prevents detriments of the same kind, for the greatest number. Since each person in a democratic society obtains the right to be free, subject only to the law of the land which protects the similar rights of others, each person may engage in an occupation, or a number of occupations, of his or her choice; may acquire assets; may travel or move from one place to another; and, subject only to lawfulness and taxation, may spend money in any conceivable transaction. In this way, people in democratic societies generally come to do those things that they are best capable of doing and both to demand and to acquire those things that they most desire to satisfy the needs of life.

Unlike pure capitalism, from which it evolved over the past few decades, free-fair capitalism requires a modest degree of governmental regulation to counteract economic disasters arising from the distinct consequences of natural disasters, unfair economic competition, or irrational economic behaviors. To be optimal in perfecting the most optimal of economic ideologies, this kind of government regulation must neither exceed nor fall short of that magnitude of implementation that becomes necessary to counteract such economic disasters. Although the history of free-fair capitalism at this time is relatively brief, the comparative prosperity of the various democratic societies into which it has been introduced to operate as a norm appears to attest to its general validity.

The most significant political event which will occur in the twenty-first century will become the single most significant event in the entire history of mankind. This event will be neither American, nor British, nor Hispanic, nor European, nor African, nor Islamic, nor Indian, nor Chinese, but universal. This event will be the political and economic unification of the human species under a world democratic federal government. The consequences of this event will include lasting peace and a greater magnitude of well-being for most of the people of the world. These benefits will derive from uniform and universal peacekeeping and law enforcement, universal disarmament, complete abolition of national armed forces, complete elimination of national military budgets, universal centralized natural disaster prediction and control, universal centralized economic regulation, the minting and circulation of a universal currency, the operations of a universal central bank, and unified efforts to synthesize and to increase the elements of human understanding.

The world democratic federal government shall be founded upon the authority of the universal social contract, the explicit agreement between each person and all other members of the human species. The social contract creates government to manage those interests which are common to everyone, which we can broadly define as the issues of personal security, social justice, and basic public infrastructure. Under the social contract, each person acquires a right to be secure against such injury as may be caused by others, and each person acquires an obligation to surrender so much personal freedom as should be necessary not to transgress against the laws of society (which, of course, will have been enacted solely to support this right). Government, representing society as the aggregate of all persons, acquires an obligation to enforce the right of each person to be secure against injury caused by others, and government acquires a right to provide personal security, social justice, and basic public infrastructure through various sovereign powers. These powers include the police power, the power of taxation, and the power of eminent domain.

The social contract shall include both the constitution of the world democratic federal government and the aggregate of all legislation enacted at each of the lower tiers of the universal government. All sections of the social contract should be expressed in language that is at once simple, clear, and readily understandable. The rationale in support of each law should likewise be clearly expressed in terms that are personal, or even psychological, so that no one can fail to understand how each law provides at the least an indirect, if not a direct, personal benefit. All laws carried over from previous periods must be reevaluated to determine whether they express a comprehensible and consentaneous rationale. Where they do not, they must be reformulated within a reasonable period of time to include such a rationale and to exclude any sections that appear to be absurd, contradictory, or irrelevant.

The universal social contract will be binding upon all persons who live within the jurisdictions of the world democratic federal government. Those persons who fail to vote in support of the inauguration of the universal democratic federation at the time of the relevant election, and those persons who reach the age of majority subsequent to that time (including, of course, all persons who will be born in later generations), having once enjoyed the obvious continuous benefits of personal security, social justice, and basic public infrastructure, will be unable to avoid being bound by the universal social contract in the same manner and to the same degree as its direct supporters. Their obligations will arise through the operation of the legal principle of quasi contract, which precludes unjust enrichment, which is to say, that it disallows persons to enjoy the benefits accruing from the execution of a contract without assuming its corollary obligations.

Salient among the numerous fundamental issues that must be satisfactorily addressed by the constitution of the world democratic federal government is the creation of the universal supreme court. This judicial body must function as the ultimate authority in the interrelated processes of administering and interpreting the laws of the society of the unified world community. Its presence, like that of a functional and independent legislature, will be indispensable for maintaining an effective crosshatch diffusion of political authority in the new universal government.

Once the history of the world democratic federal government has progressed to the beginning of its mature phase, a time when the federation will have come to comprise more than half of the nations, land area, and population of the world, its consequential benefits—lasting peace and universal well-being—will be dramatically evident. To sustain its new benefits and to prevent any possible regression of its government, the society of the unified world community will be required to introduce sweeping reforms in its public education of the young and in its social rehabilitation of convicted criminals. It will be required to introduce moral education in both arenas of public endeavor. The moral education of the young must be uniform, pervasive, and thoroughly rational. It must include the elementary theory and simple practice of courtesy at every level of human interaction. The rehabilitation of convicted criminals must feature thorough continuing moral education during the period of incarceration. Such continuing education must be expanded to a degree necessary to achieve the effective reformation of recidivists. At the same time, the society of the unified world community will need to modify its norms in such a manner as to confer its greatest honors upon its nurturers—physicians and others charged with providing health care, law enforcement officials and others charged with rehabilitating convicted criminals, and educators at all levels of service. With the passing of even one or two generations, providing that these reforms and the related changes in cultural norms have been comprehensive, complete, and thoroughgoing, crime within the society of the unified world community should greatly decrease as human happiness gradually increases.

The society of the unified world community will also need to develop a uniform legal system to supersede whichever of the four major world legal systems it may have initially adopted. We would envision that the time for the development of a universal legal system (with the period of transition from the old system(s) to the new) may be somewhat lengthy, perhaps lasting somewhere between one hundred to five hundred years, especially if the world society initially adopts both the common law and civil law legal systems.

Let us now turn to subjective symbiosism, which both facilitates and fulfills all that is useful and beneficial for human survival and well-being. Reciprocitarianism is predicated upon a principle that validates the reciprocity of benevolence and beneficence. Reciprocitarianism enables human beings to relate to each other in the optimal manner to attain the greatest emotional satisfaction. Notwithstanding that kind of reciprocity that is a prominent feature of diplomatic protocol, with its formal exchanges of courtesies and honors, reciprocitarianism is primarily a personal ethics, one that essentially applies to individuals in their private efforts to secure happiness in their lives.

Beneficial reciprocity, the activity of returning good for good, is one of six modes of interactive interpersonal behavior, others of which include beneficial initiatory behavior (the activity of initiating good towards another), detrimental initiatory behavior (initiating evil against another), detrimental reciprocity (returning evil for evil), beneficial nonreciprocity (returning good for evil), and detrimental nonreciprocity (returning evil for good). The principle of beneficial reciprocity asserts that only by initiating good towards others can we induce others to return to us in kind, thereby improving our well-being while decreasing our difficulties. The principle of beneficial reciprocity originates both in the love of children for their mothers and in the propensity of equals to cooperate with one another.

With the ascendence of egalitarianism associated with the ascendence of democracy in modern history, normal relationships between most people will be relationships between peers (with the exception of relationships between teachers and students, between physicians or other health care providers and patients, and between law enforcement officials and convicted criminals). Accordingly, four of the six traditional modes of interactive interpersonal behavior will largely disappear: detrimental nonreciprocity (except among those whose capacity to reason is either immature or severely impaired); detrimental initiatory behavior; and, with the disappearance of detrimental initiatory behavior, detrimental reciprocity and beneficial nonreciprocity. Then, the only normal relationships between most people will be those of benevolence and beneficence: beneficial initiatory behavior and beneficial reciprocity.

We can discern notable antecedents of reciprocitarianism in certain of the major world religions and in certain philosophies of ancient China. The most influential antecedent for the West is Christianity; for the East, the divergent traditions of Confucianism, Moism, and Mahayana Buddhism. But the problem of an ethics that is derived from a religion is that it ultimately depends upon the metaphysics of the religion—which is unable to be substantiated by reason. The problem of Confucianism or Moism is that either philosophy is deficient without including certain elements of the other. As an ethics, reciprocitarianism has its own rational grounds without any dependence upon metaphysics. It addresses the divergent problems of Confucianism and Moism by admitting and incorporating the better features of both philosophies.

Reciprocitarianism is the moral philosophy that is predicated upon the principle of beneficial reciprocity. We can define reciprocitarianism as that form of ethics wherein people endeavor to behave towards each other in a manner that is intended to induce beneficial reciprocity whereby to facilitate and to fulfill the satisfaction of all human needs and to provide adequate safeguards against harm.

Reciprocity in reciprocitarianism includes both the reciprocity of unequals and the reciprocity of equals. The reciprocity of unequals includes that between teachers and students, between physicians or other health care providers and patients, and between law enforcement officials and convicted criminals. This kind of reciprocity defines the relationships between the nurturers of society and those within society who temporarily depend upon the concern and the care of others. The beneficial initiatory behavior in this kind of relationship may be described as "nurture"; the beneficial reciprocity, "honor." Since the services of the nurturers of society are indispensable for society as a whole, inasmuch as all members of society, at one time or another, spend a portion of their lives as unequals among unequals, we have urged that all members of society should at all times join in conferring honor upon the nurturers of society. The reciprocity of equals include relationships that differ only in the degree of their intensity. They include one that may best be described as an introspective relationship, "self-esteem"; another, as a generic interpersonal relationship, "benevolence"; and a third, as a particular interpersonal relationship, "friendship." Self-esteem and benevolence are so clearly aligned and mutually dependent as actually to comprise an integral form of reciprocity with two hemispherical aspects—one that is introspective and one that is universal.

All forms of reciprocity in reciprocitarianism function as care. Previously, we have acknowledged that Heidegger considered care to be central to the human condition. Not only would we concur, but we would further suggest that care is central to the condition of being of all sentient life. There are four discrete aspects of care: concern (which is evident both as self-interest and as goodwill); regard (evident in self-respect, in courtesy, and in a universal esteem for the nurturers of society); justice (evident both as good faith and as fair play); and beneficence (evident in the aplomb of self-sufficiency and in acts of charity).

Friendship is the highest form of reciprocity in reciprocitarianism. Through friendship, we can correct any failures of benevolence resulting from moral dilution or inadequate reciprocal reinforcement. Through friendship, our care can deeply affect the lives of a limited number of certain other persons, the given and chosen members of our personal circles. In turn, our growing awareness of the care which certain others direct toward ourselves can deeply affect our own lives, providing us our greatest happiness by securing for us that which is most intimate and enduring in human relationships. The seven qualities of friendship (listed in the order which they might appear in the development of friendship) include understanding, encouragement, advice, apology and pardon, generosity, assistance, and, above all else, loyalty.

The practice of universal benevolence will be most effective for the members of the unified international society created by the inevitable inauguration of the coming world democratic federal government inasmuch as the traditional forms of popular particularism, predicated upon given ethnic origins, will quickly become discredited, nullified, and es-chewed in a new society constructed on a rational foundation. Until the democratic unification of the world occurs, symbiosists can best practice universal benevolence by remaining open to all human beings every-where; by condemning hubris, rudeness, and injustice wherever they ap-pear; by supporting moral education in public schools and in prisons; by promoting legislation to establish and to uphold the civil rights of the members of any as yet unprotected ethnic or demographic class; and to abide by one's moral obligations not only not to injure others but to op-pose injustice and to help others who may be in difficulty or danger at any time and place at which help for such persons can not or will not otherwise be provided.

In closing, I wish to reemphasize that symbiosism is not an original idea but a composite of the best moral ideas which mankind has as yet conceived—doing no harm; doing what is useful; maintaining goodwill; behaving towards ourselves and others with courtesy, fairness, and be-neficence; cultivating special friendships; and, when necessary and if able, being magnanimous. I wish also to acknowledge our debt to those at diverse times and places whose thought and/or example have contrib-uted so significantly to the formation and formulation of these ideas—Siddhartha Gautama, Confucius, Socrates, Mo Tzu, Aristotle, Zeno of Citium, Jesus, Marcus Aurelius, John Locke, Adam Smith, Jeremy Ben-tham, John Stuart Mill, Martin Heidegger, and Jean Paul Sartre.

The most salient quality of symbiosism is its rationality, through which it can be universally accessed and practiced. This quality enables symbiosism to surmount the intrinsic problem of religious ethics and to serve as the moral foundation of a unified world.

Symbiosism integrates objectivity and subjectivity, thereby permit-ting optimal benefits for society as a whole and for each person within it. The two realms of objectivity and subjectivity can never be mutually ex-clusive. The symbiosist essentially functions where the ethics of the two realms intersect.

Some of my readers may be inclined to conclude that the foregoing presentation of symbiosism is little more than a contemporary refine-ment, universal expansion, and necessary reformulation of eighteenth and nineteenth centuries British utilitarianism. Considered as an inde-pendent and self-sufficient moral philosophy, utilitarianism possibly could be interpreted to encompass the essential qualities of the remaining elements of symbiosism. Certainly, in and of itself, it is the most morally comprehensive of the four elements. For this reason, and to restate sym-biosism in a slightly different light, I have structured the synthesis of the philosophy with recurring suggestive references to utilitarianism. To be sure, utilitarianism encompasses the ethics of noninjury although the ethics of noninjury can not be said to comprise its major emphasis. To be sure, the heroic and humanitarian acts of the magnanimous may be said to portray the very epitome of utilitarianism although utilitarianism acknowledges that it is neither realistic nor prudent to anticipate that very many people will ever be magnanimous. It is true that John Stuart Mill distinguished between "public utility" and "private utility" but he failed to provide a full and satisfactory account of what it may mean to practice an ethics of "private utility." Of course, we can infer that the ethics of reciprocitarianism represents a feasible and an appropriate expression of an ethics of "private utility." However, as I have previously maintained, utilitarianism, at least as it historically has been defined by Bentham and J. S. Mill, is essentially and primarily an objective ethics; as such, it is fundamentally ill-suited to function as a reliable and an effective guide for the conduct and direction of one's private affairs. Accordingly, while they unquestionably share in common certain qualities, utilitarianism and reciprocitarianism in symbiosism are best considered as discrete and independent moral philosophies.

Since the ethics of symbiosism is fully rational, it belongs to the entire world. It comprises a timely and an appropriate fusion of worthy and useful moral ideas, formulated to support the approaching political and social unification of mankind. Inasmuch as it includes both objective and subjective components, it functions at the same time as a social ethics and a personal morality.

I believe that symbiosism can best be propagated by means of universal public education. Initially, the subject matter should fall under ethics; eventually, it must form a branch of an appropriate new science that can integrate the principles of psychology and sociology into a single anthropological study. Otherwise, symbiosism should not be promoted through any form of social organization. It is not a religion; therefore, periodic public worship is not necessary. It has no overriding political agenda; therefore, no political party need be formed in its behalf. Sociability and ritualism are not central to its principles; therefore, no fraternal society need be formed to advance them. To be sure, the promotion of symbiosism by any social organization apart from the school will only tend to create misunderstanding, distortion, and misapplication of its principles. Notwithstanding its unmistakable social applications in democratic government, free-fair capitalism, world federalism, and universal law, symbiosism is essentially a personal ethics. The consequences of a proper application of its principles should be no more than an improvement in the general enjoyment of life with a corollary increase in overall freedom from pain, distress, and dejection. Symbiosism, then, is merely a means to an end, and the operation of the means should be as imperceptible, undetectable, and unobtrusive as possible. In a perfect world, symbiosism would operate exclusively as a personal ethics (since the social applications of certain of its elements—democratic government, legislation and law enforcement, economic and environmental regulation, and so on—would never become necessary). Everyone would take care not to harm others, would understand where one's own freedom ends and another's begins, would consider the interests of others even while engaging in activities of self-interest. Although the world is not perfect, it is perfectible and symbiosism must still operate essentially as a personal ethics. Accordingly, it must be practiced and promoted as such, in a manner not very much unlike that of Taoism, Zen Buddhism, or Stoicism.

I will endeavor to end this discussion in the same manner that I began it, attempting to answer the parting questions of those among my readers who have graciously decided not to give up on me.

The first of their questions, "Will it not be too difficult for everyone to embrace symbiosism?" My reply, "No, not at all, since everyone enjoys pleasure just as everyone hates pain. Everyone can come to understand that one's not being injured requires that one does not injure. Everyone can come to understand how useful activity best enables one, and all, to meet the needs, and to avert the hurts, of life. Everyone can come to understand that good returns good, while evil returns evil."

Second, "In the end, will we not make golden calves of our morals?" "No, since our morals are only a means to our ends and our interest always resides in the ends."

Third, "What will become of the ethics of religion?" "They will likely persist for a very long time but ultimately they will disappear as religions become obsolete."

Fourth, "What about the ethics of radical Islamic fundamentalism?" "Any religion that openly advocates violence to achieve religious, political, or social objectives must be vigorously condemned and criminalized by all of the democratic nations. Islam in particular either must drastically reform or else become the first of the present major world religions to decline and to fall."

Finally, "Can we create a universal society of endless perfection through symbiosism?" "No, because human beings are part of nature, and nature continually evolves. We will never have a universal society of 'endless perfection' but we can have a good universal society with continuous improvement. Let us remain content with as much."

If I may have failed to answer all of the parting questions of my most loyal readers, the fault lies not in my willful neglect but in the poverty of my imagination. For this oversight, should it appear as such in the minds of even a few, and for any other shortcomings, whether apparent or not, which may impair a complete and satisfactory consideration of the ethics of symbiosism, I offer my sincere apology.

In the words of Heraclitus, "All things flow; nothing endures." There are no practical moral ideas that are fully impervious to further rational development and consequential continuous improvement. No one can enjoy a right without incurring an obligation. Any harvest that provides nourishment for all requires cultivation by all. Let those act who can not do otherwise. Let those think for whom thought comes naturally. Thought which permits universal human benefits must never be permitted to lie fallow.

# Index of General Subjects

# Index of Proper Names

# About the Author

Charles Thomas Taylor was born in 1941 in Orange, New Jersey. His earliest interests centered about classical music and by age nineteen, he had mastered piano and organ. After a number of years of teaching music to private pupils, he earned an undergraduate degree in business administration at La Salle University of Philadelphia, Pennsylvania, graduating magna cum laude in 1971. He was introduced to philosophy while a student at La Salle and he wrote his first book, *The Values*, within a four-month period immediately following his final studies there. *The Values*, a concise work of contemporary ethics, was published in 1977 by Philosophical Library of New York.

Since 1976, Mr. Taylor has been a resident of Colorado, working in the field of accounting. He is presently the Director of Finance at Airport Development Group, Inc., a small engineering and consulting firm in Denver, Colorado. He holds an M.B.A. and an M.S. in finance from the University of Colorado (1995) and became a C.P.A. in Colorado in 1997. He wrote his second book of moral philosophy, *Person and Society*, in 1998. This book was published two years later by Pentland Press of Raleigh, North Carolina.

Immediately upon completing his second book, Mr. Taylor began work on a third, *Toward World Sovereignty*, to study the benefits and problems associated with the vision of creating a universal democratic federal government. This book was completed after two years of effort, mostly on weekends and evenings, and was published in 2002 by University Press of America of Lanham, Maryland.

Mr. Taylor next turned his attention to the problem of formulating a uniform and practicable universal morality in anticipation of the potential emergence of an infant universal democratic society and government. After another two years of effort, he completed the manuscript of *Symbiosism* and is presently at work on a fifth book about the presence, use and interpretation of symbolism in various religions and works of art.